Cooking Lighthouse Style

Favorite Recipes From Coast To Coast

Frederick Stonehouse

Avery Color Studios, Inc.
Gwinn, Michigan

©2003 Avery Color Studios, Inc.

ISBN 1-892384-19-1

Library of Congress Control Number: 2002094838

First Edition 2003

Published by
Avery Color Studios, Inc.
Gwinn, Michigan 49841

Lighthouses on front cover:
Whitefish Point Light, Heceta Head Light and Cape Hatteras Light

Lighthouses on back cover:
New Presque Isle Light, Marblehead Light and Round Island Light

From the Author:

A hearty thank you to all of the individuals or organizations for the recipe contributions which made Cooking Lighthouse Style, Favorite Recipes From Coast To Coast *possible.*

Table Of Contents

Introduction

As a maritime historian I am always looking for new ways to explore sea-going history. It is like a multi-faceted diamond. As you rotate it between your fingers the perspective constantly changes as light is reflected. Each sparkle of radiance is a different aspect of the field.

While doing research on lighthouse keepers I discovered several recipes published in the old Lighthouse Service Bulletins. This sparkle of information led to the question of, "what did lighthouse keepers and their families eat?" "Was it different than the community at large?" Research showed me the answer was no, they consumed whatever people in similar geographic and economic circumstances ate. This was an interesting facet but hardly earth shattering.

While cruising through a local bookstore I noticed there were many cookbooks on the shelves as well as lighthouse books. In a flash of brilliance, (much like when peanut butter and chocolate combine to make Reese's® Pieces candy), I concluded that a lighthouse cookbook was a great concept. If I combined short lighthouse histories with recipes associated with the light or local area, it could be an excellent way to promulgate maritime history. The recipes didn't have to be historic, what a keeper and his family actually ate, but if they were at least loosely related to the lighthouse in a historic or contemporary context, the purpose would still be served. Hopefully more people would become interested in maritime history through the back door of a cookbook!

The result is *Cooking Lighthouse Style, Favorite Recipes From Coast To Coast*. Many of the recipes are indeed historic, contributed by lighthouse families. Others are contemporary, reflective of the present use of the lighthouse, perhaps as a bed and breakfast or changing culinary tastes in the area.

Purists may argue about this, saying "how can a recipe for fancy muffins served by a lighthouse bed and breakfast possibly be construed as a lighthouse recipe?" My answer is simply that lighthouses were (and still are) dynamic, always changing. As the technology of lightkeeping evolved and the actual use of the structures changed, food science transformed too. Foods undreamed of in one era became commonplace in the next. While a Lightkeeper in the 1850s may never have enjoyed fancy breakfast muffins, guests staying in the lighthouse a century and a half later find such fare very normal. Remember too, that not only did the science of lightkeeping change, but also the very use of the structures, from critical aids to safe navigation to virtual maritime monuments.

I urge you to read both the histories and learn more about these very historic lighthouses and enjoy the recipes.

Lighthouses

General

To fully understand the short lighthouse histories the reader must understand the role of the humble lighthouse in navigating American waters. The following overview should provide enough information to place the lights into an acceptable historical context. It will also show how the lights developed and operated, the personalities and organizations integral to their success and afford an understanding of the broad applications of the equipment and devices used.

Before actual lighthouses were built, local residents used various means to guide ships to safety. In 1774 one settler used a bonfire at Point Comfort to assist ships entering Hampton Roads. At nearby Cape Henry a beacon fire fueled by pine knots was kept in a large iron basket. Eventually lighthouses were built at both locations.

The first lighthouse built by the colonists was established in 1716, at Little Brewster Island at the entrance to Boston Harbor. Others soon followed. Some were erected by cities, others by merchants. Providing lighthouses was not immediately perceived as a government responsibility. Following the American Revolution the control of the lights was retained by the individual states. After the 1789 constitution, their importance was realized and the ninth law passed by Congress centralized lighthouse control under the Treasury Department. By this time there were a dozen active beacons along the east coast.

Organization

Although the lights were initially placed under the Treasury Department, the department was unprepared to manage them. Responsibility for the lights became a hot potato within the department, bouncing between different offices. In 1820, it was finally given to Stephen Pleasonton, the Fifth Auditor, who also assumed the title of General Superintendent of Lights. He kept the potato for 32 years. His duties included administering contracts, responding to Congressional inquires and generally overseeing the Lighthouse Service. Local customs collectors were given the additional job of superintending the lighthouses in their districts, including their operation and construction. Administering the lights was a thankless job for Pleasonton. A bookkeeper by profession, he had neither the maritime nor engineering background required to perform the duties in a competent manner. In addition, the position called for a man of high intelligence, great foresight and high management ability. He possessed none of these attributes, but instead seems to have been the perfect bureaucrat in the worst sense of the term. He utterly failed to realize his responsibility for the lives of ship's crews and passengers and that he owed them the best navigational aids possible. He focused only on economy and never on quality. Witnesses reported he once stated he built lighthouses cheaper than any one else and returned more money to the general fund than any other department. In all the lighthouse literature, no one has a good word to say about Stephen Pleasonton.

While significant growth occurred during the Pleasonton period, overall management was poor. The attempt was generally to spend the least possible amount of money without regard to securing acceptable equipment or results. Contracts for construction and supplies and appointing keepers were based on political affiliation, not merit. There are many instances of poor construction as shown in the large number of lights that later needed rebuilding or replacement. The outcome was a rising chorus of complaints from sailors, ship owners and insurers.

There were complaints that lights were poorly located. One Navy inspector complained that lights were "…placed in situations where the service rendered by them has not warranted the expense of their construction and maintenance." He further complained that populated coasts had many lights, while unsettled ones (and the more dangerous) had far fewer.

In 1837-38, Congress investigated the lighthouse operation and made a number of recommendations for improvement. Most of them Pleasonton ignored. Another Congressional inquiry was held in 1842, with more recommendations following. Pleasonton ignored them too!

Finally the complaints grew so loud that in 1851, Congress directed the Secretary of the Treasury to convene a special board to investigate the situation. The board's report was thorough and inclusive and concluded that the lighthouse establishment was poorly managed in both economy and efficiency. Keepers were ill-trained and in many cases incompetent and the lamps and reflectors were obsolete and inferior in design. During Pleasonton's reign the country's lighthouses were doubtless the worst in the civilized world.

Responding to the investigation, Congress in 1852, established through legislation, the nine member Lighthouse Board with the Secretary of the Treasury as ex-officio president. Other members included scientists, U.S. Army Corps of Engineers officers, U.S. Navy officers and members of the U.S. Coast Survey. The new Board organized the lights into districts and also appointed an inspector for each district, giving him the responsibility of building and maintaining the lights and equipment as well as buying supplies. The inspector was required to inspect each station in the district once every three months. As the number of lights increased, additional help was provided for the inspector. An Army Corps of Engineers officer assisted with construction and maintenance duties.

Central depots served as stationing locations for the lighthouse tenders and for storing and forwarding supplies. Repairs to the various apparatus were also accomplished by the depots trained craftsmen.

Manistee, Michigan pierhead light on Lake Michigan. Such lights were critical in providing safe harbors on the lake. Author's collection.

Improvements under the Board's leadership were significant. They established lights where needed and made certain they were well kept and reliable. Inefficient men were fired. The Board also experimented with new technology, trying whatever new equipment or fuels they thought might offer improvement. Before the advent of the Board, the U.S. provided the worst lights in the civilized world. Afterwards, we had the best. The Board also started a system of classifying lights based on the size of the lenses.

Early lightkeepers often were selected based on political loyalties. Trustworthiness, reliability or competence were not requirements; political affiliation was. Congressmen with a light in their district didn't hesitate to use the appointment of a keeper as a real plum for a deserving bootlicker. Depending on the

Lighthouses

results of an election, wholesale dismissals and appointments were made. This happened so frequently that in the interest of efficiency and economy, the Lighthouse Board had blank forms printed to use when it was necessary to notify keepers that they had been replaced!

By the late 1870s, political appointments were largely confined to the entry level positions of a third or fourth assistant keeper at the bigger lights. The keeper or first assistant were generally career positions filled by cadre personnel.

After the Civil War it was common to see veterans appointed as keepers as a reward for war service. In other instances the death of a keeper sometimes resulted in the appointment of his wife or daughter as keeper, dependent on circumstance.

The Board worked hard to get or keep good men (or women). Vacancies usually occurred only by death, resignation or dismissal. The last was invariably due to drunkenness or failure to properly keep the light. The biggest cause of keeper loss was resignation. For example, between 1885-1889, the Lighthouse Board hired 1190 new keepers and 680, or well over half, resigned. The Board was steadfast in saying that the men were not leaving because of low pay, but more likely the result of isolation and the heavy demands of the job.

The public outcry against the evils of the spoils system finally resulted in the passage by Congress in 1883, of the Pendleton Civil Service Act. Under it, appointments to key government positions would be based on ability, and special examinations were required of all applicants. Although initially only a few agencies were covered by the act, later presidents gradually increased the number. In 1896, President Cleveland added the U.S. Lighthouse Service and from then on appointments were based on merit. Following World War I, special consideration was again often given to wounded veterans, a most laudable effort on behalf of those who so bravely served.

It wasn't until 1884, that uniforms were prescribed for keepers in an attempt to create a sense of pride among the men. The uniforms were intended for official or formal occasions, such as when the inspector made his "white glove" inspection or national holidays when visitors might be expected. The first one was given to the keepers. Afterwards they were expected to purchase uniform replacements as needed. For a while the men wore regular clothing on normal workdays. Later the uniform requirement was extended to anytime the keeper was on duty. Women keepers were exempt from the uniform requirement.

To increase efficiency, in 1903, the Service was transferred to the new Department of Commerce and Labor. During the period of rapid growth, it was felt the old Lighthouse Board system of management became too cumbersome. Transfer to the new Commerce Department might rejuvenate it. It did not. In 1910, Congress abolished the Lighthouse Board and established in its stead the Bureau of Lighthouses. The new organization remained under the Commerce Department. Instead of the nine-member board, there was now only one man, the Commissioner of Lighthouses. From 1910-1935, the Commissioner was George R. Putnam, an experienced and energetic Coast and Geodetic Survey engineer. Under his remarkable leadership the new organization continued to leverage technology to improve lighthouse efficiency. An example is the use of radio beacons which became an important element of navigation safety.

The new commissioner had the authority to organize not more than 19 districts, each to be headed by a civilian inspector. An Army Corps of Engineers officer assigned to each district continued the role of providing professional expertise to lighthouse design, construction and maintenance. The entire organization was firmly under civilian control and leadership.

Growth was phenomenal. In 1852, there were 331 lighthouses and 42 lightships nation-wide. By 1910, there were 1,462 lighthouses and 51 lightships! In 1925, the system reached a total of 1,951 lighthouses, 46 lightships and 14,900 other navigational aids.

A viable retirement system for keepers was slow in coming. Often they were forced to remain in their jobs, even if old or infirm, since they had no other option. In 1916, for example, there were 92 keepers service wide over 70 years old and 24 men with over 40

The Sandy Hook *Lightship. Such vessels were an important aid to Navigation. Author's collection.*

years of service. The U.S. Life-Saving Service finally got their retirement in 1915, when they merged with the U.S. Revenue-Marine to form the Coast Guard. Three years later Congress recognized the arduous nature of the Lighthouse Service work and authorized voluntary retirement at 65 after 30 years of service and mandatory retirement at 70.

On July 7, 1939, in another move for greater governmental efficiency, President Franklin Roosevelt abolished the Bureau of Lighthouses and transferred its duties to the Coast Guard. The Coast Guard operated under the Treasury Department, so lighthouses that had started under the Treasury Department had now returned.

As part of the process of integrating into the Coast Guard, lighthouse personnel were given the option of either retaining their civilian status or converting to a military position. The integration did not go smoothly. The majority of the keepers elected to stay as civilian keepers. Many Lighthouse Service men had little desire to accept military discipline or customs. In fact, the Lighthouse Service had it's own customs and traditions and was looking forward to celebrating it's sesquicentennial on August 7, 1939, when FDR's unexpected mandate was issued. It was bitterly resented by the lighthouse community.

Construction

Usually the light station would consist of a compound of several structures: the lighthouse tower, sometimes free standing, other times integrated into the keeper's quarters, an oil house and a fog signal house. A pier with associated boathouse was also built to facilitate the landing of personnel and supplies.

Lighthouse tower heights can be very confusing. For example, Cape Hatteras is the tallest tower in the U.S. at 208 feet, but what does the height really mean? How is it measured? The tower is 193 feet from the point where the tower comes out of the ground to the vent at the top of the roof cap. It's 198 feet from the ground to the top of the lightning rod and 208 feet from sea level to the top of the tower proper. The distance from sea level to the middle of the lens, known as the focal plane, is 191 feet. So unless you are certain of what is being measured, determining the height of a lighthouse tower is always confusing.

Chicago Harbor Light. Author's collection.

Lamps, Lenses and Lights

The earliest lights used Argand lamps with parabolic reflectors. Argand lamps were developed by Aimee Argand of Geneva and used a burner with a hollow wick in a glass chimney. The first, "standard" U. S. lamp was one known as a, "Lewis" lamp. About 1812, Winslow Lewis of Massachusetts convinced his good friend Stephen Pleasonton to buy a lamp he designed and patented based on those currently in use in Europe. This was all rather strange since Lewis once stated he knew nothing about lighthouse optics! He called his device a, "magnifying and reflecting lantern," for lighthouse work, which he claimed was a combined reflector, lamp and magnifier. Later experts called it, "…as crude a device as ever emanated from the brain of an inventive man." The reflectors were made of thin copper plate with a scanty silver coating. The lens, called a magnifier by Lewis, was a circular piece of green bottle glass two and a half by four inches in diameter. One inspector said it only, "…made a bad light worse." Another testified that it was, "…worse than useless." Lewis did not argue against the criticism, but did point out the great savings in oil his device provided, using roughly half of that

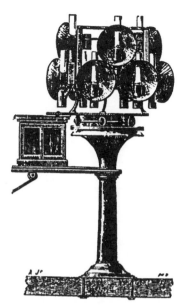

A "Lewis Lamp" style chandelier with clockworks mechanism.

of the European lamps. He had also designed his contract such that instead of money, he was paid in oil, receiving one-half of the oil his lamps saved. After the first five years of his contract, his devices had saved so much oil that the terms were changed by the government to one-third of the oil saved since the government believed it was too lucrative for Lewis! In it's basic form Winslow's device used an Argand lamp inside of a parabolic reflector with the addition of a solid piece of glass as a crude lens. To increase the power of the light and it's horizontal visibility, a number of lamps, each with it's own reflector, were mounted together in a configuration called a chandelier. A series of rings, adjustment screws and other devices were used to hold the reflectors and lamps in the correct position. It was not uncommon to find 14 or more lamps in such an unwieldy arrangement. The light at Lake Huron's Bois Blanc Island for example, had 13 separate lamps, each with a fourteen-inch reflector. The Lewis devices were complicated, inefficient and difficult to maintain. The parabolic reflectors were usually not well-made or true to form. After short use they were generally found to be bent and out of true. The silvered reflective surface in practice was scrubbed off in a matter of months because the issued cleanser was too abrasive. The lens itself attracted smoke, in turn dimming the light even more.

After the formation of the Lighthouse Board, steps were rapidly taken to equip the nation's lighthouses with the new Fresnel lens. Invented in 1820, the lens was named for Augustin Fresnel, a French scientist. Throughout it's long use as a lighthouse appliance, the Fresnel lens was constantly improved in design and performance. Without question, it was the premier lighthouse lens ever developed. These lenses have a powerful central lamp surrounded by refracting prisms and glass rings. The rings and prisms bend and guide the light, aiming it outward in powerful beams. In the old parabolic Lewis system, one half of the light was lost. In the Fresnel system the loss was less than ten per cent, resulting in an increase of over 400 per cent intensity! The Fresnel lenses were very heavy and were mounted on large iron pedestals. Weighing nearly three tons, a massive first order Fresnel lens had over 1,000 prisms. When it was necessary to revolve the light the lens was mounted on rollers or floated in a trough filled with mercury. They were so well balanced, a three ton lens could be rotated by the touch of a finger!

Augustin Fresnel, the inventor of the most famous lighthouse lens. Author's collection.

Pleasonton was absolutely against the revolutionary lens and only tested it when forced to do so by Congress. Even when it proved wildly successful he refused it's purchase. It was only with the removal of the infamous Fifth Auditor that the lens was accepted into service.

Fresnel lenses used in the United States were classified into seven sizes or orders, relating to their power. A sixth order lens was less than a foot in diameter. The largest lens, a first order, measured six feet in diameter and stood nearly 12 feet high. The lenses were also very expensive, a factor that doubtless discouraged their early adoption by the penny-pinching Pleasonton. When the United States eventually shifted to the Fresnel system it realized that as a result of their efficiency in reducing fuel costs, using only a quarter of previous amounts, they soon paid for themselves. The fuel savings resulted from usually needing only one lamp for illumination as opposed to the many required by the old Lewis system. There was also a savings in wick material and associated reflectors. Many of these wonderful lenses are now in museums where the public can view and appreciate the magnificent workmanship. Others were destroyed by vandals or official neglect when the Lighthouses were abandoned by the government.

Generally speaking, American lights burned sperm whale oil until about 1864. Two varieties were used, a thicker viscosity called, "summer oil" and a thinner variant for winter use. In colder environments, the oil had to be preheated before use to assure an even flow.

Having to warm the oil before use was often a problem, especially for a light located far out on the end of a long break water. The keeper had to carefully heat the oil ashore, then make his precarious way through storm and icy wind over a shaky wood walk way out to the light tower. Hopefully, by the time he arrived, the oil had not congealed too much for use. When the price of whale oil increased to a level the government thought too high, the fuel was switched initially to a lard oil and later to kerosene or as it was then called, mineral oil.

For a long time kerosene was thought to be too dangerous for

Fresnel lenses came in a variety of sizes or "orders." Author's collection.

lighthouse use. For example, in 1864, a Lake Michigan keeper used a kerosene lamp in his light without official approval to test it's effectiveness. For several nights it apparently worked very well, it's brilliance increasing the visibility of his light markedly. The next night it exploded, throwing oil on the keeper. A second explosion blew the lantern off the tower and shattered the lens. Eventually the problems with the volatile fuel were solved and it proved highly successful. The fuel was burned through cylindrical lamp wicks, allowing for a central flow of air for improved and cleaner combustion. Arrangements of from one to five wicks were needed to provide the necessary candlepower for a given lens. By 1886, all lamps were converted to kerosene. The amount of kerosene burned was prodigious. In 1916, over 600,000 gallons of kerosene were used in the country, more than half by the Lighthouse Service.

A massive 12-foot high first order Fresnel lens. Author's collection.

The ultimate improvement was made in 1904, when the service changed to the use of incandescent oil vapor lamps. Operating much like a Coleman lantern, fuel is forced into a vaporizer chamber and then into a mantle. This arrangement increased brilliance many times over the old-fashioned wicks. Today all lights are electric powered.

When acetylene was developed in the 1920's, it largely spelled the end for the old time lightkeepers. The flow of gas for an acetylene lamp could be regulated by a, "sun-valve" that would turn the light on and off as needed.

Fog Signals

Fog signals were also maintained at many lights. At first they were only hand rung bells, but by 1851, mechanically operated systems were in use. Later steam whistles and sirens were adopted. By 1900, nearly all fog signals were of the steam powered variety. One problem with the steam whistle, however, was the long time needed to raise the necessary steam pressure before the signal could sound. Often the process of starting a boiler fire and waiting patiently for the steam pressure to rise to a sufficient level could take as long as 45 minutes. In a busy shipping channel this was a very long time indeed. Eventually steam signals were replaced with ones using compressed air that greatly decreased response time. The compressed air was provided by gasoline or diesel engines driving special air compressors and was stored in large tanks for instant use. Regardless of the type of signal, fog still could distort sound. In some instances, a fog signal can clearly be heard five miles from the station; lost at three miles and again heard at one mile.

Operation of a steam fog-horn. Author's collection.

Flashing Lights

Developing a mechanism to make a light flash or occult, thus emitting a distinctive signal as opposed to a simple white glow, was a critical improvement to avoid confusion between lights. There were two general methods used; either to rotate the lamp and lens so that the beam was emitted only at preset intervals, or to rotate opaque panels around the lens. Power for either system came from a system of cables and weights wound to the top of the tower and allowed to slowly descend actuating a set of governing gears, much like a grandfather's clock. Every so often, usually every three or four hours, the keepers had to crank the weight back up to begin the cycle again. In some instances, colored lights, flashing or constant, were used to differentiate lights.

Daily Routine

Running a light took a special kind of person. The daily routine could be difficult and was always demanding. It also was tedious and boring, depending on one's propensity for routine and repetitive work. The light had to be maintained in a constant state of readiness. The exact details of the keeper's responsibilities could be found in the Lighthouse Board's publication *Instructions to Light-Keepers*. Virtually everything he needed to know was explained in laborious detail. The main job of the keeper was to keep the lamp burning from sunset to sunrise. To this end, *Instructions....*gave the keeper the daily responsibilities to clean and polish the lens, check and fill the oil lamp, dust the framework of the apparatus, trim the wicks and in general assure the light was ready in all regards for the next night. It is from the work of trimming the wick that

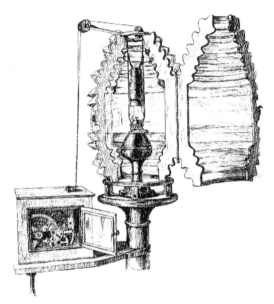

A small lens blanking or "occulting" mechanism. Author's collection.

the old keepers received the nick-name, "Wickies." Every two months he was to wash the lens with alcohol and once a year polish it with a special provided rouge. The lamps were changed every 15 days. The assistant keeper, if there was one, was tasked to clean the copper and brass fixtures of the apparatus and all tools in the lantern room as well as the walls, floors and balconies. He was to sweep the tower stairs, landing, doors, windows, recesses and passageways from the lantern to oil room. At some lights he also had to shovel the piles of dead birds off the galley deck every morning. Attracted by the bright beams, the birds were killed by the dozens when they crashed into the windows. Of course if there was no assistant at the light, the keeper had to do everything. When working in the lantern room, both men were required to wear linen aprons to prevent any chance of their coarse clothing scratching the valuable lens. Regulations called for the light to be ready for the night's use not later than 10:00 a.m. The grounds also had to be kept clean and orderly as well as all buildings and facilities. Station maintenance, including painting the tower, consumed the bulk of the men's time. Female keepers were excused from having to paint the tower.

On the sea coasts lights were exhibited year around. On the Great Lakes they were shown only during the navigation season, usually April through December.

Before *Instructions...* any training the keeper received was at best haphazard. The superintendent, (in reality the collector of customs) was supposed to instruct the new keeper in his duties, but this was not always done and was usually very rudimentary at best. If the new keeper was very lucky, the old one gave him detailed instructions before leaving. Usually this didn't happen. There was a written set of instructions that was supposed to be posted at each light, but the 1851 investigation discovered more of the stations without it than with it. This lack of adequate training and reference instructions can partially explain the disastrous condition of the lights before the era of the Lighthouse Board.

To help provide fresh vegetables, keepers often kept small gardens. Many times they were not very successful since the lights were often located in areas that did not have good soil. In some instances keepers brought boxes of their own garden soil with them. Raising chickens was also popular at many lighthouses, but there could be problems. At one station the fog horn blew so loud the chickens refused to lay eggs. At another a big wind came and just blew the chickens away, coop and all. At least the cow stayed on the ground!

The Lighthouse Service also provided special portable libraries. Packed into sets of roughly 50 books, the library boxes could easily be exchanged between stations. As an added bonus,

A mineral oil lamp is shown mounted in a third order Fresnel. Author's collection.

the boxes were designed to stack into neat bookshelves, thus helping to minimize furniture requirements. Other keepers occupied their spare time building model boats, hunting, fishing, canning, taxidermy, agate picking or mulling through correspondence courses.

The lights were supplied by special vessels called lighthouse tenders. These tough little vessels carried not only all the operating stores needed by the lights, but also the dreaded inspector. These men were infamous for their "white glove" examinations of stations. A poor inspection could spell the end of a keeper's career.

Some men handled the deadly daily routine of lightkeeping well. Others however, after a careful reading of their daily logs, appeared to, "lose their marbles." More than one keeper was driven over the edge of sanity by the terrible grinding isolation and lack of human contact.

Educating the keeper's children was frequently a problem. If feasible, the Service tried to station the keeper near to a school but many times this wasn't possible. However it is apparent the Service expended every effort to transfer keepers with families to lights close to schools. A frequent solution when schools were not available, was to board the children with a family in town. Such expenses of course were paid by the keeper, not the government.

Keepers also maintained careful logbooks of the weather, vessels passing the station and other items of daily activity. Inspectors admonished the keepers if they became too flowery or personal in their entries. After all, it was an official government journal, not a diary!

A lighthouse was often a family enterprise where the husband and wife teamed up to make the light a success. The husband as keeper assumed full responsibility for the light proper, while the wife took charge of the dwelling. The children pitched in where they could too. Everyone worked to, "keep the light."

The feared inspector was supposed to arrive unannounced, but the Service version of the, "jungle telegraph" usually gave the keepers adequate warning. When telephones were finally installed at the isolated stations a friendly call from someone at headquarters generally gave fair warning that the inspector was on his way. When one Lake Michigan inspector tried driving to some of the closer stations by car, friends of the keeper along the road also gave warning. When the inspector left the main highway and turned down the gravel road to the station someone with a telephone inevitably spotted him and called the local keeper giving him enough time for a final brush-up.

The lighthouse tender Amarnath *moored up to Detour Reef, Lake Huron. U.S. Coast Guard photo.*

If he was arriving by tender and the day was foggy, the distinctive sound of the vessel's engines revealed it's presence. In clear weather the inspector's pendant was visible on the mast.

Once the inspector was spotted, the station crew went into a flurry of activity. Last minute dusting and cleaning, straightening up and polishing were the order of the hour. Children hurried to put away toys and help wherever possible. The keeper donned his sharpest uniform and family their Sunday best. If the inspector had a weakness for hot apple pie or other baked goods, the wife did her best to whip up a fresh batch.

In the early days, keepers often moonlighted with other jobs as a way of making up for the poor pay. Fishing, farming and lumbering were popular sidelines to their official duties. As the Service matured, such practices were forbidden.

Lightkeeping was a job constantly in transition. From the free-wheeling days of the Fifth Auditor to the tight control of the Coast Guard, requirements, procedures and technology continued to evolve. The tales of the men and women that kept the lights now are only remembered in the old logbooks, yellowed news clippings and fading memories of the few old-time keepers still left. The colorful and exciting era is dead but hopefully not forgotten.

To the general public lightkeeping was a lonely and isolated job. While in reality there often was physical isolation, the keeper was usually in the midst of a technology revolution. From open fires to Lewis lamps, Fresnels, aero beacons and plastic optics; whale oil to kerosene, incandescent oil vapor, acetelyene and electricity: cannons to bells, steam whistles, air horns and radio direction signals. The roll of changes, improvements and adaptations of technology goes on and on, and keepers were in the middle of it all!

REFERENCES:

Hans Christian Adamson, *Keepers of the Lights* (New York: Greenberg, 1955), pp. 319-335.

Annual Report of the Lighthouse Board (Washington, DC: U.S. Department of the Treasury, various issues).

Captain Walter C. Capron, *The U.S. Coast Guard* (New York: Franklin Watts, Inc., 1965), pp. 121-127.

Mike Van Hoey, "Lights of the Straits," *Michigan History Magazine*, September/October, 1986, pp. 24-25.

Francis Ross Holland Jr., *America's Lighthouses, An Illustrated History* (New York: Dover Publications, 1988), pp. 1-54.

Instructions to Light-Keepers (Allen Park: Michigan: Great Lakes Lighthouse Keepers Association, 1989).

Barry James and Grant Day, *History and Archaeology of the First Copper Harbor Lighthouse*, Report of Investigations Number 21 (Archaeology Laboratory, Department of Social Sciences, Michigan Technological University, Houghton Michigan, 1995), pp. 5-32; 99.

Arnold B. Johnson, *The Modern Lighthouse Service* (Washington, DC: 1890), pp. 17-19.

Robert Erwin Johnson, *Guardians of the Sea, History of the United States Coast Guard*, 1915 to the Present (Annapolis, Maryland: Naval Institute Press, 1987), pp. 161-163.

National Maritime Initiative, Lighthouse Stations (Washington, DC: U.S. Department of the Interior, National Park Service, 1994).

Donald L. Nelson, correspondence to author, March 9, 1996.

George R. Putnam, *Lighthouses and Lightships of the United States* (New York: Houghton Mifflin Company, 1917), pp. 185-193; 196; 203; 231-232; 237-239.

Frederick A. Talbot, *Lightships and Lighthouses* (Philadelphia: J.B. Lippincott Company, 1913), pp. 29-31; 33-37;42-48; 209-210.

U.S. Department of Commerce, Lighthouse Service, *The United States Lighthouse Service, 1915* (Washington, DC: Government Printing Office, 1916), pp. 32-37; 40-56; 60-64; 73-77; 81-83.

George Weiss, *The Lighthouse Service, It's History, Activities and Organization* (Baltimore: The Johns Hopkins Press, 1916), pp. 4-10.

A.B.C. Whipple, *The Whalers* (Alexandria, Virginia: Time-Life Books, 1979), pp. 155-157.

Frederick Talbot, *Lightships and Lighthouses* (Philadelphia: J.B. Lippincott Company, 1913), p. 34.

The Great Lakes

Two Harbors Lighthouse
Two Harbors, Minnesota, Lake Superior

U.S. Coast Guard Collection

Every port on the Great Lakes had it's red light district, a place where sailors could find comfort in a shot of redeye or a roll in the hay, or both as time and money allowed. However none of the small ports was quite as open as Main Street in Two Harbors. Running from the docks to the lighthouse, it had 22 saloons and dance halls. No wonder it was called "whiskey row." Sailors, lumberjacks, iron miners and others all mixed uproariously along this infamous street.

The village of Two Harbors received its name for its proximity to two harbors: Agate Bay and Burlington Bay. The village existed for one purpose, the shipping of iron ore from the mighty Mesabi Range. Every day of the navigation season the "long ships" came to the Two Harbors docks in a never-ending stream.

The red brick lighthouse was completed in 1892. The original fourth order Fresnel lens was replaced by the Coast Guard in 1970 with an aero beacon.

Today the lighthouse is operated by the Lake County Historical Society as a bed and breakfast. Unfortunately whiskey row is long gone, done in by legions of narrow minded do-gooders intent on destroying America's colorful and rich cultural history and traditions.

Scandinavian Fruit Soup~Historic

6 cups cold water

2 cups raisins

1/2 cup dried apricots

1/2 cup cranberries

1/2 cup fresh apples, peeled and sliced

1/2 cup oranges or lemons, cut into small pieces

1/2 cup sugar

2 cinnamon sticks

1/2 cup cornstarch

Add to the cold water: raisins, dried apricots, cranberries, fresh peeled apples, oranges or lemons. Add sugar and cinnamon sticks. Cover and simmer for 30-45 minutes. Mix 1/2 cup cornstarch with 1/4 to 1/2 cup cold water, mix until it becomes smooth and add the mixture to the fruit mix. Simmer until the soup thickens. Serve warm with whipped cream. Keeps several days in the refrigerator.

Recipe Courtesy: Judy Sellman, Lake County Historical Society

Au Sable Point Lighthouse
Au Sable Point, Michigan, Lake Superior

Author's Collection

Au Sable Point has long been recognized as an extremely hazardous location on Lake Superior. As early as 1622 French voyager Pierre Radisson called it, "…most dangerous when there is any storms." The shallow sandstone reef running for nearly a mile offshore was a magnet for unwary vessels. The area was also well known for thick fogs caused by the cooler lake air intermixing with the warmer air from nearby Grand Sable Dunes. Reef, storms and fog all presented extreme perils for vessels coasting the south shore of Superior.

By the early 1870s local mariners were actively campaigning for a light at Au Sable Point. The local paper claimed, "…in all navigation of Lake Superior, there is none (coast) more dreaded than that from Whitefish Point to Grand Island." Au Sable Point is directly in this path.

Congress appropriated $40,000 in 1872 to build the light. The work progressed without undo problems and on August 19, 1874 the third order Fresnel was exhibited in the tower for the first time.

The design for Au Sable Light was not unique. The light at Outer Island in the Apostle Islands in western Lake Superior, also built in 1874, was nearly identical. Au Sable's brick tower stands 87-feet tall and is attached to the keeper's quarters by a short hallway.

Au Sable Light was one of the remote shore lights on Lake Superior. The nearest town is Grand Marais, a dozen miles to the east over a very rugged trail. It is only an eight mile run by boat, but during the depths of winter when the lake was froze solid or when gales churned the lake into a frothing maelstrom, the light is effectively isolated. One inspector commented the station is, "just as isolated as if it were thirty miles from land."

Au Sable was automated in 1958 and transferred to the General Services Administration in 1961. When the Pictured Rocks National Lakeshore was founded, the light and surrounding property was turned over to the National Park Service. Today the light station, including outbuildings, is open for tours during the summer season.

The light is still active. Although the third order Fresnel is still in the lantern room, the illumination is provided by a solar powered 300 mm lexan optic mounted outside on the galley railing.

Venison Pot Stew–Historic

Several pounds of lean Michigan venison

Seasoned flour

Beef stock or canned bouillon to cover

1 pound Michigan mushrooms, cleaned and sliced

1 cup chopped Michigan, onion

1 Michigan green pepper, chopped (remove pith and seeds)

1 cup Michigan red wine

4 or more Michigan potatoes, cubed

4 or more Michigan carrots, thickly sliced

1 can whole-kernel corn

1 or 2 peeled, cored and sliced Michigan apples (optional)

1 cup chopped celery (optional)

Likely keepers were always cautioned by the Lighthouse Board to strictly follow local fish and game regulations. Doubtless however some "deviation" occurred, enriching the lightkeeper's diet!

Cut several pounds of lean venison into 1-inch cubes and drench them in seasoned flour. In a Dutch oven or heavy kettle, melt 1/4 pound of butter and sauté the mushrooms, onion and pepper until golden brown.

Remove the vegetables from the pot and add the meat, searing it on all sides. Add more butter if necessary. Return the vegetables to the pot and add enough beef stock to almost cover the meat and vegetables. Let simmer, covered, for about 2 hours.

Add the rest of the ingredients and bring to a boil. Turn down the heat and simmer slowly until the vegetables are done.

You could add the apples and/or celery.

A dash of herbs always helps, but this recipe has the object of providing a tasty stew that retains the flavor of the venison without killing it. When the stew is done, add more seasoning if desired.

Recipe Courtesy: Michigan Department of Agriculture, http://www.mda.state.mi.us/

Big Bay Point Lighthouse
Big Bay, Michigan, Lake Superior

Avery Collection

Big Bay Lighthouse is one of the newer lights on Lake Superior. Built in 1896, it was intended to cover the dead area between the Huron Island Light, 14 miles to the west and Granite Island Light, 22 miles to the east. All were important lights to shipping, running the south coast of Lake Superior. The powerful third order Fresnel provided a light visible for 13 miles. The lighthouse is situated in a spectacular location, at the edge of a sandstone cliff high above the lake.

The red brick building is a two-story duplex that originally housed the keeper, his assistant and their families. The light was manned until 1941 when the Coast Guard automated the light and abandoned the facility. In 1961 the light station was sold to a Chicago surgeon who remodeled it extensively, making it into a private home. It later was sold to a Traverse City, Michigan businessman who used it as a corporate retreat. In 1985, the light, under new owners, became a bed and breakfast. In 1991, it was sold again, now to Jeff and Linda Gamble of Chicago and continued as a B & B.

The Gambles have worked hard to constantly upgrade and improve the facility and today it ranks as one of the most unique B & Bs in the Great Lakes. Regardless of the season, the location is breathtaking. Surrounded on the south by the deep north woods, the north is a horizon of an ever-changing panorama of Lake Superior, the greatest freshwater lake in the world.

The lighthouse also comes complete with resident ghosts. Visiting psychics claim at least six spirits make the lighthouse their home. However, the ghosts are harmless. Other than an occasional sighting of a spectral lightkeeper, they stay well out of the way.

Big Bay Light Raspberry Muffins—Contemporary

1 egg

1/2 cup milk

1/2 cup (1 stick) butter melted

1-3/4 cup unbleached flour

1/4 cup granulated sugar

2 teaspoons baking powder

1-1/2 teaspoon grated lemon peel

1/2 teaspoon salt

1 cup fresh raspberries

Heat oven to 400 degrees. Grease bottoms of 12 medium muffin cups. Using a fork, beat egg in a large bowl. Stir in milk and butter. Stir in remaining ingredients except berries just until flour is moist. Fold in berries. Divide batter evenly among muffin cups. Bake 20 minutes or until golden brown. Let stand 5 minutes before removing from pan. Cinnamon sugar can be sprinkled on muffin tops or a streusel topping added before baking. To make streusel topping, mix together 1/4 cup brown sugar, 1/4 cup chopped pecans, 2 tablespoons flour, 1 teaspoon cinnamon and 1 tablespoon soft butter. Sprinkle over muffin tops before baking. Yields 12 muffins.

Recipe Courtesy: Big Bay Point Lighthouse Bed and Breakfast, #3 Lighthouse Road, Big Bay, Michigan, http://www.bigbaylighthouse.com

Detour Reef Lighthouse
Detour Reef, Michigan, Lake Huron

Author's Collection

Detour Reef Lighthouse marks a dangerous shoal at the lower entrance of the St. Mary's River. With the increase in vessel traffic on the river and through the Soo Locks to Lake Superior, the need for safely guiding mariners grew more important.

The first light was built at Detour Point in 1847 and rebuilt in 1861. It closely resembled the light at Manitou Island on Lake Superior. A second light was constructed in 1931 on a crib directly on the reef. In design the new light very much reflected the contemporary "art deco" style. Built of steel reinforced concrete, it has a 63-foot tower topped with a third and a half order Fresnel lens transferred from the old shore light.

The light was automated in 1974. In 1998 a group of local citizens organized to assure the continuation of the light. The group obtained a long-term lease in 2000 and has made wonderful progress toward the restoration of this important Great Lake maritime landmark.

In the early fall, Detour Reef is an excellent sport fishing grounds for salmon. Native whitefish are an important local product and considered the "king" of the commercial catch.

Herbed Whitefish Paupiettes in White Wine With Cherries–Contemporary

2/3 cup pitted ripe Michigan cherries

3/4 cup dry white wine

4 whitefish fillets skinned, 6-8 ounces, each

1/3 cup minced fresh parsley leaves

1 tablespoon minced fresh thyme or 3/4 teaspoon crumbled dried

1/4 cup minced onion

2 tablespoons unsalted butter

1 tablespoon all-purpose flour

1/4 cup heavy cream

1 teaspoon fresh lemon juice

Place the cherries in a bowl and cover with the white wine. Let this mixture macerate for 1 hour. Halve the fillets lengthwise, season with salt and pepper and sprinkle the skinned side with thyme and parsley. Roll up each fillet half jelly roll style and secure with a toothpick. Repeat this process with all the remaining pieces. Stand them up in a high-sided saucepan just large enough to hold them in one layer without crowding them. Transfer the macerated cherries with a slotted spoon to a small bowl, reserving the wine. Bring the wine to a boil and pour it over the fish rolls. Cook the fish rolls, covered at a bare simmer for 8-10 minutes or until they just flake. Transfer the fish rolls with a slotted spoon to a plate, reserving the cooking liquid and keep them warm, covered.

In a small saucepan cook the onion in the butter over a moderate heat, stirring for 5 minutes, stir in the flour and cook the roux over moderately low heat, stirring for 3 minutes. Remove the pan from the heat and strain the reserved cooking liquid through a fine sieve into a pan. Add the cream, the macerated cherries, the lemon juice. Add salt and pepper to taste. Bring the mixture to a boil stirring for 3 minutes. Pour off any liquid that has accumulated on the plate, divide the fish rolls among four heated plates and spoon the sauce over them. Serves four.

Recipe Courtesy: Detour Reef Light Preservation Society, Chef Ross Kaplan

Fort Gratiot Lighthouse
Port Huron, Michigan, Lake Huron

U.S. Coast Guard Collection

Fort Gratiot Lighthouse sits at the meeting of Lake Huron and the St. Clair River connecting the upper Great Lakes with Lakes Erie and Ontario. The location has always been considered strategic by the military and shipping. In 1814 the Army established Fort Gratiot, named by the engineer in charge of construction. As shipping grew the need to improve maritime security increased and in 1823 the government appropriated money to build a lighthouse near the fort.

The infamous Winslow Lewis received the construction contract and immediately sub-contracted the project to Daniel Warren of Rochester, New York. After running over budget and getting the needed Congressional "add-ons" the light was finished in 1825 and became the first light in the State of Michigan. The tower was 32-feet tall and equipped with the standard lamps and reflectors. It was badly designed and constructed and in 1828 it toppled during a November gale.

The construction for the second tower was given to Lucius Lyon of Michigan who later would serve as a Michigan U.S. Senator. Under Lyon's direction the structure was properly built. The new tower stood 65 feet tall and is still standing! In 1857 a fourth order Fresnel lens was added.

As traffic increased the light was upgraded. In 1861 the tower was increased to 86 feet and a third order Fresnel replaced the smaller lens. When the old wooden keeper's quarters burned in 1874, a new brick duplex was built.

The great November 1913 storm nearly destroyed the lighthouse. Keeper Frank Kimball later claimed, "I watched waves as high as 30-40 feet pounding on the lighthouse and I think if the storm lasted another hour the lighthouse would have been wiped out."

The light was equipped with an aero beacon and automated in 1933.

Fort Gratiot Venison And Wild Rice Stew–Contemporary Adaptation

3-4 pounds of venison

2-1/2 quarts of water

1-1/2 cups wild rice, rinsed

2 teaspoons salt

1 cup onions

The Great Lakes region has a rich heritage of multicultural immigration, reflected in the enormous variety of ethnic cuisine available for consumption. However long before the influx of settlers from Western Europe, Native Americans populated the land. These indigenous dwellers had a healthy and simple diet based around the bountiful harvest, wildlife, fish and fresh water in abundance.

Put venison, water, salt and onion in a skillet and simmer for 1-1/2 hours, then add the wild rice and simmer for another 1-1/2 hours. Serves 4-6.

Recipe Courtesy: Barb Wilson, Contributing Editor, *Great Lakes Cruiser Magazine* and proprietor of Brandy's Tavern and Sherryl Buck.

Granite Island Lighthouse
Granite Island, Michigan, Lake Superior

Author's Collection

Granite Island Lighthouse on Lake Superior is very special among Great Lakes lighthouses in that it is privately owned. In 1999 Mr. Scott Holman, a Michigan businessman with strong connections to the Marquette area, purchased the island and its picturesque stone lighthouse. He has expended considerable resources to restore the lighthouse and remodel it into a unique private residence and retreat while still maintaining a vibrant sense of it's rich and historic maritime past.

When Mr. Holman purchased Granite Island Light Station through a General Services Administration sale, it was no bargain. Following the established procedure, the station had been offered to other agencies of the federal, state and municipal government but there were no takers. The very remoteness of the island, eight miles from Marquette, Michigan and four miles off shore, coupled with the extremely deteriorated state of the lighthouse, all conspired to scare the fainthearted away. The island is only a bare two and one half acres of rock and the little scrub vegetation present clings tenaciously to cracks in the granite.

The roof of the lighthouse had partially collapsed and virtually the entire interior was damaged by the weather. In addition, there was no landing dock on the island so bringing building supplies ashore was doubly difficult. In spite of these obstacles and many others, Mr. Holman persevered and the result speaks eloquently of his respect for Great Lakes maritime history and its adaptability for present use.

The light on Granite Island was built to cover the dead space between Marquette Harbor Light and points west for the increasingly important coast-wide trade. When the Lighthouse Board made the decision to construct the light their well-practiced engineers quickly went to work. Much of the top rock of the island was blasted off to form an area level enough to build the story and a half lighthouse. The design was taken right off the shelf and is identical to lights at Copper Harbor, Huron Islands, Sand Island (Apostle Islands) and Grand Island among other Great Lakes lights built during the same general period. In the spring of 1869 the construction crew and materials arrived on the lighthouse tender *Haze*. The deep water around the island allowed the tender to ease in close to the rocky shore and boom the supplies ashore. A small railway was built to cart the supplies from the shore to the construction site.

Life at Granite Island was generally uneventful. Storms came and went damaging the station and requiring periodic repair. As at all lights, maintenance was a constant need. Tragedy struck on August 30, 1872 when keeper Isaac P. Bridges drowned when his boat capsized in rough water en route to the island from the mainland. His family watched in horror as he perished!

The light was automated in 1939.

Civet de Lapin (Granite Island Lightkeeper's Rabbit Stew)–Historic

6 tablespoons sweet butter

18 small onions

1/2 pound bacon cut in pieces

1 three-pound Granite Island jackrabbit

1/2 cup white flour

1 tablespoon salt

1 teaspoon black pepper

1 tablespoon chopped garlic

1 cup chicken broth

2 cups dry white wine

1 bay leaf

1 tablespoon dry thyme or branch of fresh thyme

12 small new potatoes from assistant's garden

1 stalk celery cut in small pieces

Melt butter in pot. Add onions, bacon and cook until done. Roll the rabbit pieces in flour, salt and pepper and add to pot after removing the bacon and the onions. Brown over a quick fire 5 minutes, turning the pieces often so each one will get brown on all sides. Add the garlic, stir well on the fire, 2 minutes, add the onions, the bacon and flour that remains after drudging the rabbit. Mix well over fire one minute, pour chicken broth and white wine.

Add the bay leaf and thyme. Let cook slowly 45 minutes covered. Add potatoes and celery, check the seasoning and continue cooking for 35 minutes. Remove bay leaf before serving. Sauce should be smooth and thick.

Recipe Courtesy: Martine Holman, Granite Island Light Station, www.graniteisland.com

Harbor Beach Lighthouse
Harbor Beach, Michigan, Lake Huron

Harbor Beach Lighthouse Society Photo

In the early days of Great Lakes navigation, the Lake Huron waters between Port Huron and Saginaw Bay were empty of all shelter. If a vessel got into trouble during a northeast gale, there was nowhere to run. Vessel owners and mariners lobbied Congress for aid and the U.S. Army Corps of Engineers was eventually directed to construct a harbor of refuge at Sand Harbor, today's Harbor Beach. Work started in 1873 and finished in 1885 when a long system of piers was finished. The project cost nearly $1 million, a massive sum for the times.

A lighthouse was built on a crib at the end of the north pier to guide ships into the new harbor. Constructed ashore, the crib was floated out and sunk into position by filling it with rocks until it was fast to the bottom. A 45-foot conical iron tower was then built on the crib, which is actually just off the pier and connected with a short walkway. A fourth order Fresnel lens was installed in the lantern room.

In 1986 the Fresnel lens was replaced with a 190 mm optic and the original lens loaned to the Harbor Beach Historical Society. It is on display at the Grice Museum, conveniently located near the public marina.

Heath® Bar Coffee Cake–Contemporary

2 cups brown sugar (crust use)

2 cups flour (crust use)

1 stick butter (crust use)

1 beaten egg

1 cup buttermilk

1 teaspoon vanilla

1 teaspoon soda

Pinch salt

6 Heath® bars

Cool Whip®

Mix crust ingredients like a piecrust; reserve 1 cup for topping. Add to the remaining, 1 beaten egg, 1 cup buttermilk, 1 teaspoon vanilla, 1 teaspoon soda, pinch of salt, mix by hand just until the ingredients are damp. Pour into greased pan, sprinkle with reserved cup of topping. Break up 6 Heath® bars and sprinkle over top, sprinkle with nuts, if desired. Bake 350 degrees for 30-35 minutes in 9" by 13" pan. Add Cool Whip® for topping.

Recipe Courtesy: Karen Kadar, Harbor Beach Lighthouse

Huron Island Lighthouse
Huron Island, Michigan, Lake Superior

Huron Island Lighthouse Preservation Association Photo

Huron Island Lighthouse is typical of the many small coastal and harbor lighthouses built on the Great Lakes in the latter 1860s. Simple in design and function, the design proved one of the best ever developed by the Lighthouse Board.

The Huron Islands are a group of eight small islands totaling 147 acres. Mostly rock, they offer no home to anything but birds and in the case of Lighthouse Island, rabbits too! The rabbits were more help than hindrance. Sometimes at the end of a season, when the keepers were waiting for calm weather to leave the light for the winter and supplies were low, the men lived on rabbit and beans! The islands were never settled other than the minor civilization offered by the lighthouse keepers and their families. Today the inhabitants are limited to eagles, piggish cormorants, sea gulls (locally known as "dump eagles") and other birds. The islands were designated a National Wildlife Sanctuary in 1905 by President Theodore Roosevelt. Today they are part of the Huron National Wildlife Refuge and managed as a satellite of the Seney National Wildlife Refuge.

As ship traffic increased along the south shore of Lake Superior the need for a light on the Huron Islands became more important. The Lighthouse Board noted that, the islands "are a constant source of anxiety to navigators, wrecks having frequently occurred at this point."

The lighthouse at the Huron Islands was built at the same time as the one at Granite Island and first illuminated on October 28, 1868 using a third and half order Fresnel lens.

While the lighthouse certainly prevented many wrecks, it didn't halt them all. During a blinding snowstorm on April 30, 1909 the tow barge *George Nestor* wrecked on the cliffs just below the light. Keeper Frank Witte and his assistant Casper Kuhn attempted to save the seven-man crew but were unable to do so. The men died before their eyes.

The waters surrounding the islands are excellent fishing grounds. Legend claims it was common for some of the keepers to sneak out with the station boat under-cover of fog and pilfer fish from the nearby commercial gill nets. As long as they didn't get too greedy, the loss was never noticed. The men also did not always pay the strictest attention to state game laws. It was rumored they occasionally did a little "poaching" on the mainland. Some visitors to the island remembered that some of the beef served had a distinct taste of venison.

Today the Huron Island Lighthouse Preservation Association, a volunteer group, is working hard to restore the lighthouse, which has suffered badly from decades of official neglect.

Skanee Apple Pie-Historic

5-6 large tart apples, best if picked from Skanee, Michigan

1/4 cup brown sugar

3/4 cup granulated sugar

1/4 cup flour

1 tablespoon cinnamon

1/2 teaspoon nutmeg

1/4-1/3 cup butter

Ingredients to make piecrust or pre-made crusts (Betty Crocker piecrust recipe for 2 10-inch pie crusts)

This recipe originally came from Laura Collins, the daughter of James Collins, one of the Huron Island lightkeepers. During the summer the family often stayed at the light but in the fall moved back to their home on the lakeshore at Skanee. The apples came from the local orchards. The pie was always a lighthouse favorite.

Preheat oven to 425 degrees. Peel, core, quarter and slice the apples. Set in salt water until ready to put into plate. Make the piecrust. Line the bottom of a 10-inch pie plate with 1/2 of crust rolled out to about 1/4-inch thick. Place about 3/4 of the apples in the plate. Sprinkle with a mixture of half the sugars. Fill the pie plate with the rest of the apples and sugar. Sprinkle with the cinnamon, nutmeg and flour. Place pats of butter around the top of the apples. Cover with the other crust and seal the edges of the pie. Slit the top of the crust at about 1 to 2 inch intervals.

Bake at 425 degrees for 15 minutes, then reduce heat to 400 degrees for 45 minutes. The pie is baked when juice starts to run out of the top of the pie. Hint: by placing the pie plate on a cookie sheet while baking, you can avoid having the juice running over and burning the oven.

Recipe Courtesy: Chris Collins, Huron Island Lighthouse Preservation Association

Manitou Island Lighthouse
Manitou Island, Michigan, Lake Superior

U.S. Coast Guard Collection

Located at the tip of Lake Superior's infamous Keweenaw Peninsula, Manitou Island Lighthouse has a colorful history. The peninsula juts out into the lake like a boney finger of death. All vessel traffic bound to and from the western lake must round the rock-studded point. During the preceding two centuries perhaps 100 ships have wrecked in the area, from striking reefs and shoals, colliding with each other in the fog or overwhelmed by storm. The little lighthouse on Manitou Island doubtless saved many others from similar fates.

The first lighthouse was established in 1850. Poorly constructed it was replaced with the current structure in 1861. The 80-foot skeletal iron tower is identical to that at Whitefish Point also erected in 1861.

There are two fascinating incidents associated with Manitou Light. Keeping a light in a remote area like Manitou Island was always difficult, not only for the keeper but also for his family. The following journal entry by keeper James Corgan for July 15, 1875 illustrated the point. "Principal keeper started out at 8:00 P.M. in the station boat with wife for Copper Harbor in anticipation of an increase soon after arriving. When one and a half miles east of Horseshoe Harbor, Mrs. Corgan gave birth to a rollicking boy; all things lovely, had everything comfortable aboard. Sea a dead calm."

In 1884 Keeper Nathaniel Fadden reportedly manufactured whiskey at the lighthouse and sold the resulting product to the local Indians. Because of the remote location, his activities were not immediately noticed. However when the Indians, angry over the quality and price attacked the lighthouse, the situation rapidly got out of hand. The result was the dismissal of keeper Fadden.

Indian Trade Whiskey–Historic

1 handful red peppers

1 quart black molasses

River water as required

1 quart alcohol

1 pound rank black chewing tobacco

1 bottle Jamaica Ginger

Using alcohol in the Indian trade was a popular practice working to the great advantage of European traders. The Federal government had laws making it illegal to sell alcohol to the Indians but there was too much money involved to easily stop the trade. Certainly Keeper Fadden was just following this long tradition. Indian whiskey was also known as firewater, coffin varnish, dirt cutter, fool's water, white mile and dynamite. Some variations even included gunpowder! All were designed to deliver the greatest possible punch to the consumer at the least cost and allow the trader to take maximum advantage of the resulting condition.

The pepper and tobacco were blended together. When cool other ingredients were added and stirred. As the Indians became drunk, more water was added.

Recipe Courtesy: Old Lightkeeper

Marquette Lighthouse
Marquette, Michigan, Lake Superior

Brandon Stonehouse Photo

The original lighthouse at Marquette was built in 1853. Like many of the lighthouses of that era, it was poorly constructed and soon needed replacement. The present brick lighthouse was built in 1866. A second story was added in 1906 to provide quarters for the assistant keeper, who had been living in a renovated barn. The addition of the second story to this common design makes the structure unique among Great Lakes lighthouses.

The Marquette light was one of the most important on Lake Superior. Although comparatively small, and exhibiting only a fourth order Fresnel, it was the critical navigational aid for the iron ore freighters entering Marquette harbor. For a century following its founding in 1849, Marquette was the principal iron ore port on the Great Lakes. Throughout the Industrial Revolution, it was Marquette iron that provided the muscle for the expanding national economy. Generations of Great Lakes sailors used the light to help them make a safe trip. Marquette is still a major iron ore shipping port.

The 40 foot tower is 77 feet above the water and provides a spectacular view of the shoreline. The lighthouse is also the oldest major building in the city, the rest having been destroyed in a devastating fire in 1886.

The lighthouse is currently leased by the Marquette Maritime Museum and is undergoing restoration into a lighthouse museum.

Upper Peninsula Pasty-Historic

Crust:

3 cups flour

1/4 cup lard

1 cup finely ground suet

6-7 tablespoons cold water

1 teaspoon salt

Filling:

1 pound beef, cubed or diced, good quality

1/2 pound pork, cubed or diced, good quality

Potatoes

Turnip

Onion

Butter

Parsley

Carrots, finely grated

Long a favorite of the Cornwall area of England, the pasty came to Michigan when the Cornish miners arrived in the 1850s to develop the rich iron and copper deposits of the Upper Peninsula. It quickly became a favorite dish.

Recipes vary, as with any food preparation and everyone in the Upper Peninsula will have their own favorite. This recipe was common to Marquette circa 1900.

Blend lard into flour, preferably with pastry blender. Add suet which has been finely ground. Work in thoroughly with flour mixture. Add cold water to make soft dough, just a little bit moister that ordinary pastry dough but not as soft as biscuit dough. Divide dough into four pieces and roll each piece out to the size of a dinner plate. On one half of the rolled out dough build up the ingredients as follows: A half-inch layer of finely chopped potatoes; season with salt and pepper. Follow with a thin layer of sliced turnips, then a very thin layer of chopped onion, carrots and sprinkle in parsley. Cover with about one fourth of mixed cubed beef and pork and season once more. Top with piece of butter about the size of a walnut. Now fold uncovered portion of dough over filled portion and crimp edges. Your pasty is now somewhat in the shape of a half moon. Make a one-inch slit in the top of the dough and place prepared pasty on a greased cookie sheet or a pie pan and put in the oven. Bake at about 400 degrees for an hour.

Recipe Courtesy: Marquette County History Museum, Marquette, Michigan 49855, http://www.marquettecohistory.org

New Presque Isle Lighthouse
Presque Isle, Michigan, Lake Huron

Avery Collection

New Presque Isle Lighthouse was constructed in 1870 as a replacement for the 1840 Old Presque Isle Light a mile to the south. The brick tower stands 100 feet high, making it one of the tallest on the Great Lakes. A story and a half keeper's quarters is attached.

When the new lighthouse was finished the keeper from the old light, Patrick Garrity, transferred to it. Certainly he was pleased to move his family into the larger and newer quarters. Garrity had been a keeper since 1861 and he kept the new light until 1885 when he retired and his son, Thomas, took over the job. The son was a real lighthouse man, staying at the light until his retirement in 1935, a fifty-year tenure! Lightkeeping must have run in the family. For many years a daughter, Anna, kept the local range lights.

Presque Isle Lighthouse also has a ghost story. The tale goes that a keeper (not Garrity) would lock his wife in the tower when he went to town to visit his girlfriend. As he left the grounds, his wife would yell her curses at him from the galley high on the tower. In time he grew tired of her nagging and murdered her, burying her body in the thick woods. To explain her absence, he claimed she went home to her parents. Today some people claim her spirit remains in the tower and it is said when the wind blows hard from the right direction, her curses can still be heard echoing over the grounds.

The Presque Isle Lighthouse is part of a county park and the third order Fresnel lens is still in the tower.

Early Colonial Bread—Historic

1/2 cup yellow cornmeal

1/3 cup brown sugar

1 tablespoon salt

2 cups boiling water

1/4 cup cooking oil

2 packages active dry yeast

1/2 cup lukewarm water

3/4 cup stirred whole wheat flour

1/2 cup sifted all-purpose flour

4-1/4 - 4-1/2 cups sifted all-purpose flour

Thoroughly combine the cornmeal, brown sugar, salt, boiling water and oil. Let cool to lukewarm, about 30 minutes. Soften the yeast in the 1/2 cup lukewarm water. Stir into the cornmeal mixture. Add the whole wheat and all-purpose flour; mix well. Stir in enough all-purpose flour to cover surface and knead until smooth and elastic, 6-8 minutes. Place in greased bowl, turning once to grease surface. Cover and let rise in warm place till double, about 50-60 minutes.

Punch down; turn out on lightly floured surface and divide in 1/2. Cover and let rest 10 minutes. Shape into two loaves and place in greased 9 x 5 x 3 inch loaf pans. Let rise again until almost double, about 30 minutes. Bake in 375 degree oven for 45 minutes or until done. Cover loosely with foil after first 25 minutes if bread browns rapidly. Cool on rack. Make 2 loaves.

Recipe Courtesy: Kammie Dennis, Presque Isle County Tourism

Point Au Barques Lighthouse
Point Au Barques, Michigan, Lake Huron

Avery Collection

Point Au Barques marks the area where Lake Huron meets Saginaw Bay. It is thought the name refers to the stopping place used by early fur traders. As described in the *Great Lakes Pilot*, it is an extremely hazardous area. "A dangerous reef with rocks covered by less than 6 feet near its outer edge extends 2 miles east from Point Au Barques Light." The light was built in 1847 to warn mariners clear of the reef. It was rebuilt ten years later. The 89-foot brick tower had a third order Fresnel and cast a beacon visible for 15 miles.

In 1876 a U.S. Life-Saving Station was added to the point. They quickly proved their worth, saving many shipwreck victims. Including the crew of the big steel steamer *Howard M. Hanna* wrecked on the reef during the infamous November 1913 storm. This single storm wrecked 17 vessels, 11 of them modern steel freighters lost with all hands and killed 250 sailors. In April 1879, the life-saving crew was nearly wiped out in a terrible disaster. Seven of the eight-man crew were killed in an effort to reach a storm stressed schooner. The men of the old Life-Saving Service lived their motto: "Regulations say we have to go out. They say nothing about coming back."

In 1958 the land and lighthouse were sold to Huron County and is presently a maritime museum and park. The light is still active with an automatic aero beacon instead of the classical Fresnel lens.

Point au Barques Soup a 'l 'Oignon (French Onion Soup)–Contemporary Adaptation

4 tablespoons butter

2 tablespoons vegetable oil

3 pounds onions, thinly sliced (about 7 cups)

1 teaspoon salt

3 tablespoons flour

2 quarts beef stock, fresh or canned (can also use a combination of beef/ chicken stock)

The sweeping impact of the early French voyageurs on this beautiful part of Michigan is shown in many ways. One of the most delicious is the lingering influence of French-influenced cuisine, flavored with tasty herbs and spices and savory stocks.

In a heavy 5-quart saucepan, melt the butter with the oil over moderate heat. Stir in the onions and 1 teaspoon salt and cook uncovered over low heat, stirring occasionally for 20-30 minutes or until the onions are a rich golden brown. Sprinkle flour over the onions and cook, stirring for 2-3 minutes. Remove the pan from the heat. In a separate saucepan, bring the stock to a simmer, and then stir the hot stock into the onions. Return the soup to a low heat and simmer partially covered, for another 30-40 minutes, occasionally skimming off the fat. Season to taste. Serves 6-8.

Recipe Courtesy: Barb Wilson, contributing editor for *Great Lakes Cruiser Magazine* and proprietor of Brandy's Tavern.

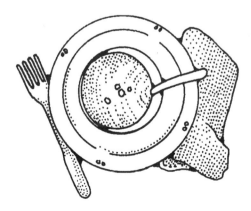

Rock Of Ages Lighthouse
Isle Royale, Michigan, Lake Superior

U.S. Coast Guard Collection

When Rock of Ages Light was first exhibited on October 26, 1908 it was one of the last built on the Great Lakes. Because of its remote location, the construction was extremely difficult and the eventual success was heralded as a major engineering feat. The light was intended to aid vessels to clear the rocks at the southwest tip of Isle Royale. During the fall many vessels bound to and from Duluth, Minnesota or Superior, Wisconsin took shelter from the strong northerly winds by running a course along the shore north and in the lee of Isle Royale when the lake was too rough for the shorter southerly track.

The light is built on a rock 50 feet wide and 210 feet long, jutting a bare sixteen feet above the water. The cylindrical tower is constructed of brick with concrete trim and a steel skeletal framework. The second order Fresnel lens, with a focal plane of 117 feet, flashed at an estimated 940,000 candlepower, visible on a clear day for a distance of 19 miles.

Rock of Ages Reef was the site of three major shipwrecks, the steamer *Henry Chisholm* in 1898, side-wheeler *Cumberland* in 1875 and big steel passenger steamer *George M. Cox* in 1933. When the *Cox* struck the reef, the fog was so thick the captain was unable to see the lighthouse. However the Lightkeeper, high in the lantern room saw the twin masts of the steamer heading directly for the rocks. Although he frantically blew his fog signal, the *Cox* never altered course and slammed into the reef at full speed, ramming 110-feet of the vessel clear of the water! Eventually all 121 passengers and crew were rescued.

Poached Whitefish–Historic

4 Whitefish fillets or whole cleaned whitefish

4 cups water, boiling

1 small onion, chopped

1/2 teaspoon thyme

1 bay leaf

3 cloves garlic, chopped

1/2 teaspoon basil

1/2 teaspoon sage

1 tablespoon lemon juice

1 small red pepper, diced

Minced parsley

4 small-medium potatoes cut into chunks (optional)

1 large carrot, sliced (optional)

1 stalk celery, sliced (optional)

This recipe is from the Sivertson family, one of the original Isle Royale fishing families. The Sivertsons still hold a life lease on property near the Rock of Ages Light and remain very active in commercial fishing on Lake Superior. Members of the family assisted in the rescue of victims from shipwrecks on the reef.

Rinse fish thoroughly in cold water. If using whole fish, score back of fish with small slices. To the boiling water add onion, thyme, bay leaf, garlic, basil, sage, lemon juice and red pepper. Let boil thoroughly for about 10 minutes, and then gently place fish in water (to avoid breaking). Simmer fish 10 minutes and remove from water. Drain, lay on a platter, garnish with minced parsley and serve with drawn butter.

The celery, carrots and potatoes are optional. They can be added to the poaching water with the spices and served as a side dish with the fish.

Recipe Courtesy: Lake Superior Fish Company, 1507 North 1st Street, Superior, Wisconsin 54880-1146

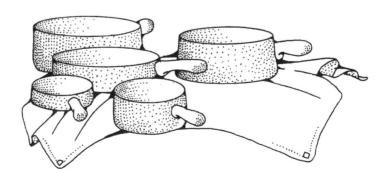

Round Island Lighthouse
Round Island, Michigan, Lake Huron

Avery Collection

The Straits of Mackinac is an extremely hazardous area for shipping, especially in the days before Global Positioning Systems, radio, radar and other electronic aids. The many shoals, reefs and sand bars lay in deadly wait for captains who wander off course.

During the hey day of Great Lakes shipping, Round Island Light was an important aid to navigation. In 1894 Congress provided $15,000 to construct a lighthouse on Round Island located just to the south of Mackinac Island and five miles east of the Straits.

The resulting lighthouse was a three-story brick building with attached tower. A fourth order Fresnel lens provided the beacon.

The light was automated in 1924 and keepers removed. In 1947 a tower light was built on the breakwater at Mackinac Island largely replacing the Round Island Light. The island was absorbed into the Hiawatha National Forest in 1958. Ignored by the government, the lighthouse rapidly deteriorated, suffering from the elements and vandals. A storm in 1972 washed away a corner of the building.

Fearing the entire structure would collapse and very concerned with the impression the crumbling lighthouse was making on visitors to the world famous Mackinac Island, a local group formed to save the old light. By 1973 work was in full swing and over the years tremendous progress was accomplished. It is still serving as an active light with a 300 mm optic in the tower instead of the Fresnel lens. Round Island is certainly one of the most photographed lights on the Great Lakes, considering that every ferry to and from Mackinac Island passes close aboard the light.

Mackinac Island's unique environment has a special turn of the century atmosphere. Transportation is limited to horses, bicycles and walking. There are no motorized vehicles allowed. Since the 1870s the island has been a favorite vacation spot for people from throughout the country.

Round Island Mackinac Chocolate Fudge–Contemporary

3 cups sugar

3/4 cup butter

2/3 cup evaporated milk

1 12 ounce package chocolate chips

7 ounces marshmallow cream

1 cup chopped nuts (optional)

1 teaspoon vanilla

When the resort era began on Mackinac Island in the 1870s there were many small candy shops. As time passed, the tourist sweet-tooth shifted from the appeal of general candies towards fudge. Before long, fudge in many varieties became a staple of the shops, each claiming to have the "best" fudge on the island. Many of the shops feature fudge making in front of tourists, with large vats of fudge cooking, then poured on marble slabs and finally worked and cut in front of the customer. This rich recipe will certainly provide the "Mackinac Island" experience.

Combine sugar, butter and milk in heavy 2-1/2 quart saucepan. Bring to a full rolling boil over medium heat for 5 minutes, stirring constantly to prevent scorching. Remove from heat, stir in chocolate until melted. Add marshmallow cream, nuts and vanilla. Beat until well blended. Pour into a buttered 9 x 13 inch pan. Cool. Cut into squares.

Recipe Courtesy: Linda Franks, Michigan Reflections, http://members.tripod.com/~fin-man_2/index-1.html

Sand Hills Lighthouse
Five-Mile Point, Michigan, Lake Superior

Sand Hills Lighthouse Photo

Sand Hills Lighthouse holds the distinction of being the last and the largest of the land-based lights built on the Great Lakes. Located at Five Mile Point on the shores of the scenic Keweenaw Peninsula, the station presents an unusual appearance. It is a massive squared off three-story structure with a seven-story lighthouse in the middle. Made of steel framing and reinforced concrete with a cream-colored brick facade, it is in stark contrast to the "normal" lighthouse.

A light at Eagle River had protected the western side of the Keweenaw, four miles to the northeast of Five Mile Point. The small Eagle River Light was built in 1854 to guide vessels into Eagle River, an early copper mining port. The Keweenaw Peninsula contains some of the richest deposits of native copper in the world. Following its discovery in 1844, the Keweenaw blossomed with the deep shaft mines and belching smelters. Soon ships were clogging the ports to carry the copper to market. By 1892 however, Eagle River had silted up and was no longer useable. The Lighthouse Board recommended discontinuing the light and shifting it to Five Mile Point. Finally in 1908 the light was extinguished for the last time but it was not until 1917 that Congress appropriated $70,000 for the new light. Meanwhile the coast remained unprotected, with expensive results. About five miles offshore is a long series of reefs known as Sawtooth Reef. Over the years many ships have died on it's grinding teeth but most famous is the brand new steel freighter William C. Moreland, driving up on the rocks in November 1910. Deaf to the pleas of shippers, the stretch of coast remained dark.

Construction finally started in April 1918. Since there was no road access, the materials and workers all came ashore on two hastily built docks. The work went fast and the new light was in business on June 18, 1919. A fourth order Fresnel was used in the tower.

Part of the reason for the larger size of the lighthouse was that it contained three apartments, providing space for the keeper plus two assistants. A large fog house was built near the lakeshore. Reportedly it had the loudest horns on the Great Lakes. Life at the lighthouse continued without change until 1939 when it was automated.

During World War II, the station was reactivated as a Coast Guard boot camp. Up to 200 men at a time trained at the lighthouse, many housed in the converted barn. In 1954 the station was abandoned and the light discontinued. Declared surplus by the Coast Guard, it was sold to a private party.

Today the Sand Hills Lighthouse has been restored to its former glory and operates as a magnificent bed and breakfast.

Hot Fudge Brownies–Contemporary

5 ounces unsweetened chocolate

2/3 cup butter

3 eggs

1-3/4 cup granulated sugar

2 teaspoons vanilla extract

1 cup flour

1 cup walnuts, finely chopped

Hot Fudge Sauce:

1 package Hersheys® Classic Caramels

8 ounces milk chocolate

1 teaspoon vanilla

1 cup French vanilla ice cream

Melt unsweetened chocolate and butter over low heat. Combine the eggs, sugar and vanilla and beat at high speed for 5 minutes, then add chocolate/butter mixture and combine thoroughly.

Add flour and walnuts and mix thoroughly and spread into greased 9 x 9 inch pan. Bake at 350º for 40 minutes. Cut into 16 squares.

To make hot fudge, heat caramels until melted in a double boiler. When melted, stir in 8 ounces milk chocolate and 1 teaspoon vanilla. When the chocolate is melted add the ice cream. Blend thoroughly until ice cream is melted.

Serve the brownies in bowls floating them in the hot fudge topping. Place a scoop of French vanilla ice cream on top of each brownie. Then a generous spoonful of fresh whipped cream and top with a maraschino cherry.

Recipe Courtesy: Sand Hills Lighthouse Bed and Breakfast, Ahmeek, Michigan 49901, 906-337-1744

Sand Point Lighthouse
Escanaba, Michigan, Lake Michigan

Author's Collection

The design of the Sand Point Lighthouse in Escanaba, Michigan is identical to many small Great Lakes harbor lights; a brick one and a half story building with attached tower and fourth order lens. But unlike any other Great Lakes light, the contractor erected it backwards, facing away from the harbor!

In the 1860s Escanaba was rapidly growing into a major shipping point for lumber and iron ore. More and more vessels were entering and leaving the harbor and a light was needed to guide the ships around the shoals of Sand Point.

The lighthouse was built in 1867 at a cost of $11,000. John Terry was appointed as keeper however he died before the light became operational and his wife Mary assumed his job. She proved a capable and well-liked keeper until the night of March 4, 1886 when a mysterious fire swept through the building. There was much speculation as to its cause. A lengthy coroners jury returned the conclusion she died under unknown conditions. Some townspeople believed she was a victim of robbers. Did she discover them and was then knocked unconscious in the ensuing scuffle? Did the murders set the fire to cover the crime? Another theory held that the fire started in the oil room and Mary was overcome by smoke. The mystery of her death was never solved.

Today the lighthouse is no longer in use as an aid to navigation. A new off shore crib light has taken over as the beacon for ships rounding Sand Point. The Delta County Historical Society currently operates the lighthouse as a museum. It is a wonderful example of our Great Lakes maritime past.

Sand Point Honey Substitute–Historic

6 cups of sugar

1-1/2 cups water

Scant 1/2 teaspoon alum

A dozen or so wild rose petals

1-1/2 teacups full of white clover crowns

1 teacup full of red clover crowns.

The rocky shores of Lake Michigan blossom with wild roses and clover in early summer and these are the secret ingredients used to transform simple into "honey."

Prepare four small canning jars and keep them warm. Slowly boil the sugar and water for eight minutes. Add alum and cook for one minute more. Remove from the heat and add petals and crowns while stirring gently. Allow them to steep for five minutes before straining the mixture directly into the hot jars. Seal immediately and enjoy all year.

Recipe Courtesy: Sand Point Lighthouse, Delta Historical Society, P.O. Box 484, Escanaba, Michigan 49829

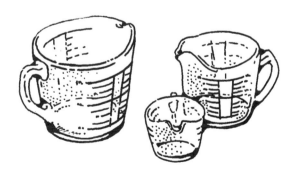

Seul Choix Lighthouse
Seul Choix Point, Michigan, Lake Michigan

Gulliver Historical Society Photo

Seul Choix Point Lighthouse is one of the most beautiful lighthouses on the Great Lakes. When first illuminated on September 5, 1895, it was graced with an attention to detail not typical of the Lighthouse Service. A glance at the top of the 78-foot brick tower or the peak of the quarters building clearly shows the uniqueness of the light.

Seul Choix Point Lighthouse (pronounced Sis Shwa) translates in French as "only choice." During the days of the French voyageurs, Seul Choix harbor, about 60 miles west of the Straits of Mackinac, was a favorite stopping point when Lake Michigan turned ugly. The men also found the waters around Seul Choix were rich with fish and eventually a small fishing community started based around their small "only choice" harbor. As shipping increased, the waters off the point were recognized as a significant danger. A long reef extends off the point and vessels needed to steer clear lest they rip their bottoms off on the sharp rocks. In addition, the point was in the middle of a 100-mile stretch of wild and unsettled coast without a guiding light.

In response to these problems, Congress appropriated $15,000 in 1886 to build the light. The work however was delayed for various reasons and even after it's completion in 1892, had to be rebuilt due to inferior materials. A third order Fresnel was installed in the lantern room but was later replaced with a modern aero beacon. The light was automated in 1972 and is still an active aid.

Today the light station, including foghorn building, is operated as a museum by the Gulliver Historical Society. The volunteer group has done a wonderful job of restoring the lighthouse to its former glory.

The lighthouse is also reportedly home to well documented supernatural activity. Popular belief holds Captain Joseph Townshend, a former keeper who died in the lighthouse, responsible. They believe his spirit still wanders the house and grounds. Many visitors claim to have experienced his chilling presence.

Broiled Whitefish With Lemon Butter–Historic

3 pounds whitefish fillets

Olive oil

Salt and pepper to taste

1 cup butter

2-3 tablespoons freshly squeezed lemon juice

1/2 teaspoons pepper

1/4 cup parsley, chopped

1 teaspoon dried tarragon leaves

1 dash Tabasco sauce

Flour

Water

Great Lakes whitefish have long been prized for the delectable quality of their meat. One early scientist stated, "We can say from personal experience that a diet of whitefish along with no other food, can be eaten for days without losing its appeal." The fish school in the cold, deep waters and are still plentiful in Lake Superior, northern Lake Michigan and Huron.

Season fillets with salt and pepper; rub oil over both sides. Place on broiler rack 5 inches below heat source and broil 5 minutes on each side. To prepare sauce let butter soften at room temperature. Melt butter in small saucepan. Stir in lemon juice, pepper, parsley, and Tabasco sauce. Whisk together until blended. Mix small amount of flour with water until smooth; stir sauce to thicken.

Recipe Courtesy: Marilyn Fischer, Gulliver Historical Society, Gulliver, Michigan 49840

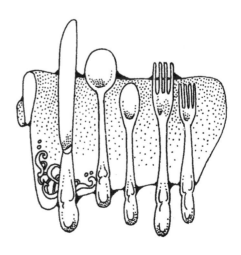

South Manitou Island Lighthouse
South Manitou Island, Michigan, Lake Michigan

Author's Collection

The original lighthouse at South Manitou Island was a story and a half brick building with a wooden tower protruding through the roof in the style of the early Cape Cod lights, it was erected in 1840. The first keeper also ran the island's thriving wharf and cordwood business. Apparently he spent more time running his business than operating the light. He also lived over a mile distant and hired a man to run the light. The beacon was also partially obscured by trees and two of the lamps were facing inward toward land where they did no good at all. The Lake Michigan inspector received enough complaints that the keeper was eventually removed.

Regardless of the problems with the keeper, the lighthouse itself was flawed and a replacement was built in 1858. The new tower was still too short and the present 104-foot brick tower was built in 1871 and connected to the 1858 quarters with a long hallway. A third order Fresnel was mounted in the lantern room. Mariners considered the new tower, one of the tallest on the Great Lakes and more powerful lens, a great improvement to lake commerce.

Manitou Island Light was critically important. It helped guide ships through the infamous Manitou Passage. This shipping channel was (and still is) a short cut for vessels running between the Straits of Mackinac and lower lakes ports such as Chicago and Milwaukee among others. To date, the reefs and shoals of the Passage have wrecked an estimated 50 ships. The light also helped guide ships into South Manitou Harbor, an important fueling stop for wood burning steamers.

South Manitou Island is about nine miles off the Michigan coast and five miles south of its sister North Manitou Island. Barely four by four miles, it was considered a very agreeable assignment for keepers and their families.

On March 15, 1878 the light was the scene of a terrible tragedy. Keeper Aaron Sheridan, his wife and infant were in a small sailboat with a friend when a sudden squall capsized the craft. When the boat went over the boom apparently struck Sheridan in his head knocking him out since he never surfaced. His wife, holding the child to her chest, desperately grasped the bottom of the boat. Before the friend could tie her and the child off, she lost her grip and drowned. What makes this disaster doubly tragic is the older Sheridan children watched the entire drama from shore!

The Coast Guard discontinued the light in 1958. A dozen years later the property passed to the National Park Service becoming part of the Sleeping Bear Dunes National Lakeshore.

Manitou Chicken and Noodles—Historic

1 whole chicken or chicken parts with skin and fat attached

2 cups flour

1 egg

1/4 teaspoon salt

2 tablespoons milk/water

1 onion, if desired

James and Lillian Burdick and their children raised chickens on South Manitou Island. There are wonderful photographs in the Visitor's Center on South Manitou Island of the family on a porch with chickens pecking in the foreground. James was the second assistant keeper 1901-02 and first assistant 1908-28.

1. Slowly cook chicken in water/broth until tender. Debone. Set chicken aside and cover. Reserve the liquid.

2. Mix flour, egg, milk/water, and salt. Knead mixture until the dough pulls away.

3. Roll dough to desired thickness (Note: It will fatten when cooked).

   3a. Allow to dry on counter then cut into noodles.

   3b. Cut into noodles using pasta maker and allow to dry on rack.

4. Return liquid to a boil; add onion if desired. Add noodles slowly, keeping the liquid boiling.

5. Cook until desired tenderness achieved, 20-30 minutes.

6. Add chicken and serve. Serves 4-6.

Recipe Courtesy: Margaret Braden, grandniece of James and Lillian Braden

Stannard's Rock Lighthouse
Stannard's Rock, Michigan, Lake Superior

Mark Yankovitch Photo

The old lightkeepers called Stannard's Rock the "Loneliest Place in America" and with good reason. Located 44 miles off Marquette, Michigan, it is the most distant light station from land of any in North America.

The story began in 1835 when Captain Benjamin Stannard discovered a reef in what could be called the middle of Lake Superior and dangerously close to shipping lanes. The need for a lighthouse was apparent but it wasn't until 1877 that the Lighthouse Board felt capable of building the tower. When the second order Fresnel lens was first exhibited on July 4, 1882, it marked the completion of what was the most difficult and expensive lighthouse construction on the Great Lakes. The new 110 foot limestone tower stood in tribute to their skill. Over a quarter million tons of iron, steel, concrete and rock went into the structure.

Stannard's Rock light was tremendously strong to withstand the awesome power of Lake Superior storms and ice. During roaring northwest tempests, 35 foot waves slammed into the tower, shaking goods off shelves and sending spray over the top of the lantern room. Winter ice drove hard against the concrete crib. Some years it was over 40 feet thick when the keepers arrived in the spring. Stannard's Rock, often just called the "Rock" by the keepers, was always a stag station. Families were never allowed at the light.

The keepers endured incredible loneliness. Some men could take it and others could not. One assistant lasted a bare week before quitting. Others withstood the desolation for longer periods, but in the end were driven away by the empty horizons, pounding waves and screaming winds. One keeper, overwhelmed by the emptiness, was reputedly carried off the light in a straight jacket and directly into the local hospital's mental ward. In spite of such stories, other men thrived at the Rock. Keeper Louis Wilk once spent a record 99 continuous days on duty, a testament to dedication.

In June 1961, a terrible explosion shook the tower. The exact cause was never determined, but likely a gasoline generator exploded. One of the three Coast Guard keepers was killed outright, literally blown to kingdom come. Others were injured.

The Coast Guard automated the light in 1962 and it is still an active aid although now a lexan optic is used instead of the old lens. The twelve bulls eye Fresnel, the largest lens ever used on the Great Lakes, is on display at the Marquette Maritime Museum.

Rock Ginger Bread–Historic

1/2 cup shortening

1/2 cup butter

1/2 cup sugar

1 egg, beaten

1 cup molasses

1-1/2 teaspoons soda

1 teaspoon cinnamon

1/2 teaspoon clover

2-1/2 cups flour

1 teaspoon salt

1 cup hot water

Stannard's Rock Reef is likely the most productive Lake Trout fishing area in the Great Lakes. Before regulation, commercial fishing vessels made regular stops to load their boats. Today it is a popular destination for sport fisherman anxious to experience the thrill of catching lunker trout on light spin tackle.

Doubtless however the old keepers grew just a mite tired of fish and a loaf of home baked ginger bread was a real morale boost.

Cream shortening and butter, add sugar. Add beaten egg, molasses and the dry ingredients. Add hot water last and beat until smooth. Bake in a greased 9-inch by 13 inch pan. Heat oven to 350 degrees. Bake 40-45 minutes or until tooth-pick comes out clean.

Recipe Courtesy: Linda Franks, Michigan Reflections

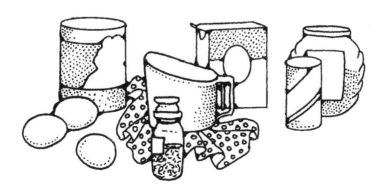

St. Helena Island Lighthouse
St. Helena Island, Michigan, Lake Michigan

Terry Pepper Photo

Located four miles west of the Straits of Mackinac, St. Helena Light has long been an important aid for vessels running between Lakes Huron and Michigan. First operated in 1873, its 71-foot brick tower was topped with a third and a half order Fresnel lens. An attached story and a half keeper's house was also constructed. The island isn't very large, only about a mile long and 3/8 mile wide. Why it was named St. Helena is a bit of a mystery. Originally known as St. Helene, it was later anglicized to Helena. The French voyageurs called it Isle St. Helene.

The light was automated in 1923 when an innovative acetylene lamp was installed. The design used two metal rods that would expand when the sun heated them in turn cutting off the gas supply and extinguishing the light. When the sun set, the rods cooled and expanded, turning on the gas and igniting the light.

In February 1913 the keeper distinguished himself when he saved the lives of two fishermen lost on the ice in a blizzard. Northern Lake Michigan typically froze in the winter and it was common for people to travel by sleigh between St. Helena and the village of St. Ignace, four miles to the east.

In 1986 the Great Lakes Lighthouse Keepers Association obtained a thirty-year lease from the Coast Guard and began the difficult job of restoring the light. After the 1923 automation, the lighthouse was boarded up and virtually abandoned by the government. Vandalism and general deterioration were extreme. Through broad based community support including the active help of several Boy Scout troops, the lighthouse has been magnificently restored and stands as a tribute to the members of this fine organization.

Welcome Mints–Historic

3-4 mint leaves

3 cups confectioners powdered sugar

2 tablespoons butter

Red or green food coloring as desired

2 tablespoons cold water

Welcome mints are one of the specialties at St. Helena Island Light Station. During the summer, a plant from the square stemmed mint family covers the limestone shoreline with a floral display of tiny purple flowers. Every time visitors walk in this area, the brisk breeze of the Straits carries the minty aroma through the windows of the lighthouse dwelling.

When visitors are expected, it is time to make welcome mints. Take a leisurely walk out the summer kitchen door, around the corner and into the herb garden. Upon reaching the limestone marker labeled "spearmint" remove 3 or 4 nice leaves from the domestic plant mint and return to the summer kitchen. Using a sharp knife mince the leaves into small pieces. Using a small stoneware bowl, measure 3 cups of confectioners powdered sugar. Using a wooden spoon fashioned from the gnarl of a white cedar tree mix in 2 tablespoons of very soft butter and the minced mint leaves. Slowly add approximately 2 tablespoons cold well water. You might want to add red or green food coloring to the water, if color is desired. Knead the dough with your hands, adding a little more water, or a little more powdered sugar, to obtain a smooth soft consistency. The dough should not be too dry to fall apart nor too moist to stick to your hands. Taking a small section of the dough, mould it into a marble sized sphere. Then flatten the dough between your fingers to 1/4 inch thick. Place the welcome mints on a cut glass plate. The recipe makes about 3 dozen mints. Serve the incoming guests and enjoy their company. It might be days before visitors arrive from the mainland.

Recipe Courtesy: *Summer Kitchen Recipes From the St. Helena Island Lighthouse,* Great Lakes Lighthouse Keepers Association

Waugoshance Lighthouse
Waugoshance Point, Michigan, Lake Michigan

Waugoshance Lighthouse Preservation Society Photo

For a time during the last part of the 19th Century, Waugoshance Lighthouse was one of the most important lights on the Great Lakes, marking the critical turning point for vessels running from the Straits of Mackinac along the east shore of Lake Michigan. Inward of the light is an eight mile long stretch of deadly shoals and reefs. If the mariner turned too soon, destruction was certain. Even if they made the correct turn, the water still ran shallow. It was adequate for the early days of lake navigation, but too shallow for newer freighters. They had to continue further west into deeper water. As the growth in ship size made the light obsolete, it was discontinued in 1912.

In 1832 a lightship was stationed at Waugoshance and remained until the first lighthouse was finished in 1851. The light was the first one on the Great Lakes built using a submerged crib. The conical brick tower stands 76 feet high and is capped with an iron bird cage lantern room, a type rare on the Great Lakes. Eventually a fourth order Fresnel replaced the old lamps and reflectors.

For additional weather protection it was encased in iron sheeting in 1883. In 1912 it was discontinued when the new White Shoal Light, four miles to the northwest became operational.

There is an unstated reason for the closure, namely that the ghost of a former keeper made the light uninhabitable for the living keepers. The tale goes that in 1900 keeper John Herman was a well-known prankster. John was also a drinker, especially on leave. Supposedly John returned to the light from leave in an intoxicated and playful condition. For unknown reasons he locked his assistant in the tower. In spite of the man's shouts, John never responded. In desperation the assistant used a rope to climb down to the crib. The keeper was gone! The only conclusion was that John fell off the crib into the water and drowned. Ever since the keepers were bedeviled by super-natural activity. Doors would open and close, common items disappear only to reappear later. It was all a repetition of the pranks John used to pull. Because of this unnatural activity, it became increasingly difficult to find men willing to serve at the light. Eventually it got to the point that it was easier to discontinue the light rather than keep it.

During World War II the lighthouse was a training target for strafing by naval aviators. Bullets and decades of neglect have seriously damaged the old light. The Waugoshance Lighthouse Preservation Society is now working to save this important early lighthouse.

Waugoshance Clafoutis aux Cerises (Cherry Cake)–Contemporary Adaptation

4 eggs

1/2 cup all purpose flour

1-1/2 cups milk

1/4 cup sugar

2 teaspoons vanilla extract

2-3 cups fresh black sweet cherries, pitted (can also use canned Bing cherries, drained and pitted or frozen sweet cherries, thawed and drained)

Confectioners (powdered) sugar

The northwest area of Michigan's Lower Peninsula has long been famous for the bountiful cherry crops produced there. In recent years the harvest has expanded to include award-winning vineyards. Even in earlier times, a variety of simple, tasty ingredients were available for the wife of the Waugoshance lightkeeper to bake a cherry cake.

Preheat the oven to 350 degrees. Stir the flour and eggs together in a large mixing bowl and slowly stir in the milk, sugar and vanilla extract. Beat with a whisk, rotary or electric beater until the flour lumps disappear and the batter is smooth.

To prepare the batter using a blender, combine the milk, eggs, flour, sugar and vanilla in the blender and blend at high speed for a few seconds. Turn off and scrape down the side of the blender with a rubber spatula, then blend again for approximately 40 seconds.

Pat the cherries completely dry with paper towels then spread them evenly in a shallow, buttered 13" x 9" x 2" baking pan. Pour in batter. Bake on the middle shelf in the oven for 1-1/2 hours or until the top is golden brown and firm to the touch. Dust lightly with confectioners sugar and serve while still warm. Serves 4-6.

Recipe Courtesy: Barb Wilson, Contributing Editor, *Great Lakes Cruiser Magazine* and proprietor of Brandy's Tavern and Sherryl Buck

Whitefish Point Lighthouse
Whitefish Point, Michigan, Lake Superior

Avery Collection

The need for a light at Whitefish Point was long known by mariners who sailed the big lake, more formally called Lake Superior. But it took newspaper publisher Horace Greeley to clearly state the pressing need. During a trip on Superior in June 1847 he wrote, "Congress has ordered a lighthouse to be erected here, a commissioner has located it, yet every months delay is virtual manslaughter."

Whitefish Point is particularly dangerous for shipping since it is the turning point for vessels entering and leaving Whitefish Bay. It is a choke point in the classic sense! It is also one of the most tremendous places for storms. The prevailing northwest storms can build over hundreds of miles, slamming waves into the sandy point with ferocious furry.

Pea soup fogs only made shipping congestion all the more horrific, especially in the days before radar. The offshore waters soon gained the name, "the graveyard of Lake Superior." Today there are an estimated 100 shipwrecks in the area. Among the wrecks is that of the 729-foot *Edmund Fitzgerald*, lost with all 29 hands during a vicious November 10, 1975 storm. By any standard, there was a desperate need for a light at Whitefish Point.

The lighthouse was eventually built by Ebenezer Warner in 1848 and first illuminated in the spring of 1849. The 65-foot tower was made of broken stone and topped with an iron lantern room containing 13 lamps with 14-inch reflectors.

Fueled by the opening of the great Marquette Iron Range and Keweenaw copper mines of Michigan's Upper Peninsula and the 1855 opening of the Soo Canal, vessel traffic around Whitefish Point boomed. As the stream of upbound and downbound vessels grew, so did the importance of the light at Whitefish Point.

Ebenezer's tower didn't stand the test of time and in 1861 the current 76-foot iron pile tower was erected. The original clockworks mechanism used to cause the light to flash, was a very inferior design. It had to be wound every hour, which proved too much work for a single keeper and allowed him to argue successfully with the Board for an assistant keeper.

Today the Whitefish Point light and the lighthouse are part of the Great Lakes Shipwreck Historical Society Museum; a world-class facility that draws rave reviews from visitors.

Cranberry Waldorf Salad–Contemporary Recipe

2 cups fresh cranberries, ground

1/3 cup honey

2 cups chopped, unpeeled tart apples

1 cup seedless green grape halves

1/2 cup chopped English walnuts

1/4 teaspoon salt

1 cup whipping cream, whipped

Cranberries have been raised commercially at Whitefish Point from the 1870s. For the people that lived along this desolate part of the Lake Superior coast, marketing the berries provided an important source of extra income during the long cold winters.

Combine the cranberries with the honey in a bowl and mix well. Chill, covered, for 8-10 hours.

Add the apples, grapes, walnuts and salt to the cranberries and mix well. Fold the whipped cream into the salad. Spoon into a salad bowl. Chill for several hours. Garnish with green grape clusters and whole fresh cranberries. Yield: 8 servings.

Recipe Courtesy: Jan M. Holt, *Treasured Recipes From the Shipwreck Coast*, Great Lakes Shipwreck Historical Society, Sault Ste. Marie, Michigan, 1996.

Charlotte-Genesee Lighthouse
Charlotte, New York, Lake Ontario

U.S. Coast Guard Collection

The Charlotte-Genesee Lighthouse is one of those lights that by all rights should have been destroyed generations ago but the spirit of the local community kept it alive. The light was built in 1822 on a bluff overlooking the mouth of the Genesee River as it flowed into Lake Ontario. At the time Genesee was becoming an important shipping town and a good lighthouse was necessary for it to continue to grow. The 40-foot, octagonal tower is made of rough limestone and supported a ten-sided lantern room. The original keeper's house was rebuilt in 1863 into a two story red brick structure.

As lake shipping increased in vessel size and cargo carried, it gradually outgrew the little harbor at Genesee and in 1881 the light was discontinued, although lighthouse and later Coast Guard personnel continued to use the quarters. When the Coast Guard decided to demolish the unused light, a letter writing campaign by local high school students convinced the Coast Guard to reverse its decision. In 1965 the Charlotte-Genesee Lighthouse Historical Society assumed control of the lighthouse. By this time the iron lantern room was missing, apparently removed for use elsewhere. Again the high school students came to the rescue and fabricated a new one. Today the second oldest lighthouse on the Great Lakes is back again to its old glory and in full operation as a maritime museum.

Catfish Soup—Historic

2 large or 4 small catfish

1 pound lean bacon

1 onion

3 teaspoons parsley

4 egg yolks

1 tablespoon butter

2 tablespoons flour

1/2 pint half and half

Salt and pepper

What could be better on a cold blustery fall day than a rich bowl of catfish soup? This basic recipe can be made with many varieties of fish and is equally good.

Clean catfish, cut off heads and skin. Cut each into 3 parts. Perch or other fish may be used. Place fish in pot with bacon, cut up onion, parsley, pepper and salt. Cover with water. Stew until fish are tender but not broken. Beat yolks of 4 eggs and add butter, flour and half and half. Heat and add to soup to thicken. Serve.

Recipe Courtesy: Old Lightkeeper

Dunkirk Lighthouse
Point Gratiot, New York, Lake Erie

U.S. Coast Guard Collection

Like many lighthouses, the original lighthouse at Dunkirk fell victim to shoreline erosion. It was constructed in 1827 to guide ships into Dunkirk Harbor. The red-bricked tower was rebuilt 50 years later but the lake continued to move closer. The Lighthouse Board built the current tower and keeper's quarters in 1876 at a safe distance from the shore.

An iron lantern room tops the square 61-foot tower while the keeper's house is high Victorian gothic in style. A third order Fresnel lens provided a beam visible for 15 miles. Dunkirk was considered the most prominent light on the south shore of Lake Erie.

The waters off Dunkirk are home to many shipwrecks. Notable among them is the steamer *Erie*, burning in 1841 with the loss of 141 lives. The disastrous fire was apparently caused by the storage of highly flammable paint and kerosene directly over the red-hot boilers! In 1897 the steamer *Idaho* foundered with cargo of general freight, much of which washed ashore in front of the lighthouse, including slabs of chocolate.

Today the lighthouse is a military museum, with rooms dedicated to each service as well as Vietnam and lightkeeping.

Ship's Potato Salad–Historic

25 pounds potatoes, freshly boiled

4 quarts celery, diced

1-1/2 cups onions, minced

36 eggs

3/4 cup salt

3/4 tablespoon pepper

9 tablespoons celery seed

1/2 pint vinegar

3/4 pint salad oil

2 quarts mayonnaise

6 heads lettuce

Cook potatoes in skins. Peel and slice while warm.
Dice celery.
Mince Onions.
Hard cook eggs and chop.
Spread layer of potatoes in bottom of shallow baking pan.
Mix salt, pepper, celery seed, vinegar and salad oil together; sprinkle over sliced potatoes in bottom of baking pan. Repeat, filling pan with alternating layers of potatoes and oil mixture. Allow to stand 1 hour.
Combine celery, onions, eggs and mayonnaise.
Add potatoes; mix well.
Chill and serve on crisp lettuce leaves.
Yield: 100 servings

Recipe Courtesy: *Cooking and Baking on Shipboard*, War Shipping Administration, Washington, DC, 1945

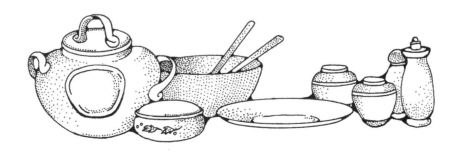

Fort Niagara Lighthouse
Niagara, New York, Lake Ontario

U.S. Coast Guard Collection

The first lighthouse on the Great Lakes was erected at Fort Niagara in 1781. The French built the fort at the mouth of the Niagara River in 1726, an important stopping point for fur traders. The British captured the fort in 1750 during the French and Indian War. Since the harbor at Niagara was good, when vessel traffic on Lake Ontario increased, a light was considered necessary.

The first light was not a freestanding tower but rather just a small lantern room built on the roof of one of the fort's buildings. With few ships on the lake, the light was discontinued by the Americans in 1796 and the tower taken down. When commerce increased, a second wood tower was built on the roof in 1823. This light lasted for 50 years. During this period, commerce slowly declined. The Erie Canal and Welland Canal, built in 1825 and 1829 respectively, allowed vessels to bypass the Niagara River so a proper lighthouse was not needed.

The present lighthouse was established in 1872. It had a 50-foot octagonal stone tower with attached workroom. A fourth order Fresnel was used in the tower. It is a beautiful light, befitting its inherited role as the first light on the Great Lakes. In 1900 the tower was extended by 11 feet, but instead of continuing the original stone courses, yellow brick was substituted as an economic move.

The light was transferred to a new tower in 1993 and the old tower is now dark. However it is leased to the old Fort Niagara Historical Association and operated as a museum and gift shop.

Baked Kippered Herring–Historic

7-1/2 pounds kippered herring

1 ounce lemon juice

1/2 cup butter

1/4 cup parsley

1/2 cup onions, chopped fine

1 teaspoon pepper

Water

Herring, whether from the Atlantic or Great Lakes, can be a tasty dish, especially after a hard day at the lighthouse.

Soak kippered herring 10 minutes in enough boiling water to cover. Drain. Place herring on baking sheets in even rows. Combine lemon juice, butter, parsley, finely chopped onion and pepper. Pour just enough water on bottom of pan to keep the herring moist while baking. Bake in hot oven (400 degrees F.) about 10 minutes. Garnish with lemon and serve. Yield: 25 servings.

Recipe Courtesy: *Cooking and Baking on Shipboard*, War Shipping Administration, Washington, DC, 1945

Selkirk Lighthouse
Selkirk, New York, Lake Ontario

U.S. Coast Guard Collection

Selkirk Lighthouse at the mouth of the Salmon River was erected in 1838. The two-story building is made of chocolate colored stone and the wooden tower projects through the roof at the north end. A very rare "bird cage" lantern room is still on the tower. The light marked the entrance to the harbor, which was becoming an increasingly important trade center. The lighthouse is one of only four ever constructed from this particular design and is the best surviving example of the type.

The first permanent settlement was established in the district in 1801. The local salmon fishing was an important economic attraction as was the rich farmland. Later during the War of 1812 it was a haven for smugglers. Although there is some dispute, Selkirk was likely named for the Earl of Selkirk who had extensive land holdings in the area in the 1790s.

In keeping with available technology the original lighting apparatus was a set of 14-inch reflectors and lamps. In 1855 the light was upgraded to a sixth order Fresnel. After a general decline in trade, the light was discontinued in 1858.

In 1895 it was purchased by a hotelier and converted into a successful resort complex. Capitalizing on the miles of sandy beaches, lake vistas and excellent fishing, it soon became a very popular destination. During prohibition, it again was popular with smugglers.

In 1989 the light was returned to the tower when a Class II private navigation aid was added. Today Selkirk Lighthouse continues its historic mission and plans are in place to restore it to its former 1838 glory. Today it is available for rent as a housekeeping unit, in keeping with the resort tradition of the area.

Fisherman's Rice Casserole–Contemporary

2 cups cooked rice

1-1/2 cups sliced celery

1 can (6 ounces) olives, sliced

2 tablespoons sliced onion

1 cup mayo

1/2 cup green onion

1 can (7 ounces) tuna, drained and flaked

1 can (4-1/2 ounces) shrimp, drained and rinsed

Flavored almonds, optional

Combine all ingredients except seafood and almonds, mix well. Fold in tuna and shrimp. Spoon into shallow 1-1/2 quart casserole dish. Cover with almonds. Bake at 325 degrees for 25-30 minutes until heated.

Recipe Courtesy: Nicole Paternoster, Selkirk Lighthouse Marina Crew, 6 Lake Road Extension, P.O. Box 228, Pulaski, NY 13142-0228

Sodus Point Lighthouse
Sodus, New York, Lake Ontario

U.S. Coast Guard Collection

Sodus Bay was once a very busy shipping community. In the early years of Great Lakes development a parade of vessels freighted lumber, grain, block ice and coal from the harbor. In addition, a fleet of tugs carried on a lively fishing trade and small shipbuilders turned out a long stream of schooners and small steamers. Excursion vessels carried a flood of tourists over the bay and surrounding waters.

After being petitioned by ship owners and mariners, Congress appropriated $4,500 to construct a conical stone light tower and keeper's house. By 1869 both 1825 structures were in sad repair and funds were provided to build a new lighthouse. Both were finished on June 30, 1871. The new lighthouse was made of limestone imported from Kingston, Ontario and had an attached square tower containing a fourth order Fresnel lens. The stone from the old tower was used to build a small jetty in front of the new light.

Sodus Light was discontinued in 1901 when local marine traffic decreased. Sodus harbor was always small and ship size had dramatically increased. As the lake commerce moved westward, Sodus was left behind. A small beacon light placed on the west pier was sufficient for local vessels.

From 1901-1984, the old house was used as quarters for the personnel maintaining the pier light. Today the lighthouse is maintained as a museum by the Sodus Bay Historical Society.

Apple Crisp–Contemporary

5 large apples

1 cup sugar

3/4 cup flour

1 egg

1 teaspoons baking powder

3 tablespoons butter

Apple Crisp is always a great desert, especially when the sharp chill of fall is in the air and the trees have turned into a riot of reds and yellows.

Slice apples and place in greased 8" baking dish. Combine sugar, flour, egg, and baking powder. Mix well, until crumbly. Sprinkle over apples. Melt butter and pour over topping. Bake at 350 degrees for 35 minutes.

Recipe Courtesy: Carriage House Inn, Sodus Point, NY, www.Carriage-House-Inn.com

Erie Land Lighthouse
Erie, Pennsylvania, Lake Erie

U.S. Coast Guard Collection

The first light at Erie, Pennsylvania, a small 20-foot tower, was built overlooking the harbor in 1818. Stability problems with the tower necessitated the construction of a new 56-foot tower in 1858. This tower was also unstable. Later testing revealed a deep layer of quicksand, which allowed the tower to shift, providing a poor foundation. A third 49-foot sandstone tower was finally built on solid ground in 1869. A keeper's residence was built two years before.

The 1869 tower was used until 1881 when the Lighthouse Board discontinued it and sold the property. Four years later the Board reversed itself and bought the property back. The tower was raised 17 feet in 1897 to clear the trees that had grown around the light but two years later it was permanently discontinued. The valuable lantern room and third order Fresnel lens were removed with the lens going to Marblehead, Ohio and the cage to the local lighthouse depot.

The property was transferred to the City of Erie in 1934 as part of a park complex. In 1989 a wooden lantern room was built to complete the appearance of the light.

Ginger Snap Cookies–Historic

1 cup sugar

3/4 cup shortening

1 egg

1/4 cup molasses

2 cup sifted flour

2 teaspoons baking soda

1/4 teaspoon salt

1 teaspoon cinnamon

1 teaspoon ginger

Ginger snap cookies are an old American favorite. In some sea-faring families it was believed the ginger would ward off sea sickness!

Cream sugar and shortening. Add the egg and molasses and beat well. Add sifted flour, baking soda, salt, cinnamon and ginger and mix. Chill dough for several hours. Roll into small balls, dip in sugar, place on greased cookie sheet and flatten. Bake at 375 for 15 minutes. Makes about four dozen cookies.

Recipe Courtesy: Old Lightkeeper

Fairport Harbor Lighthouse
Fairport, Ohio, Lake Erie

U.S. Coast Guard Collection

The first light at Fairport Harbor was built in 1825 and had a full career before being replaced in 1871. The original tower stood 30 feet high, capped with an eight-sided iron lantern room. The light was necessary due to the increased traffic on Lake Erie and growth of Fairport Harbor. In 1847 alone nearly 3,000 vessels called at Fairport carrying nearly a million dollars in cargo. Not only did the light perform the traditional task of serving as beacon for ships, but in the years before the Civil War also was a layover in the Underground Railroad. For the slaves fleeing the South, it was a last stop before reaching safety in Canada. The fugitives were hidden in the cellar beneath the keeper's house until it was time to spirit them across the lake.

After the War, it was apparent the old lighthouse was too far-gone. Poor construction, the effects of weather and a crumbling foundation all meant a new light was needed. When the replacement light was finished in 1871, the new gray sandstone tower measured 60-feet high. A two story brick keeper's quarters was attached. The lens was a third order Fresnel.

When the Coast Guard relocated the light to the new breakwater, it decided in 1925 to demolish the old tower. A vigorous campaign by the community prevented such cultural desecration. In 1945 ownership of the light passed to the city of Fairport.

Today the Old Fairport Harbor Lighthouse is a maritime museum featuring exhibits on life-saving, maritime charts and lighthouse artifacts among others. When it opened in 1946, it was the first maritime museum in Ohio and the first lighthouse museum on the Great Lakes. The present light is pictured.

Lake Erie Fried Fish–Contemporary & Famous Lake Erie Perch–Historic

Fillets (or nuggets) of perch or walleye, well dried with paper towel

Batter:

1 cup flour with dash of salt

1/2 teaspoon baking powder

1/2 teaspoon baking soda

1/2 cup vinegar

1/2 cup water

Lake Erie Fried Fish

Fried fish is a very popular Lake Erie dish and everyone seems to have their favorite recipe. This one is guaranteed to make your mouth water.

Dip fish in batter, covering well and deep fry.

Recipe Courtesy: Chargin Lagoons Yacht Club

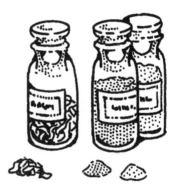

Fillets (or nuggets) of perch or walleye, well dried with paper towel

1 cup flour

2 beaten eggs

Bread crumbs

Famous Lake Erie Perch–Historic

Wash Lake Erie perch fillets, dip in flour, then into beaten eggs and coat with seasoned bread crumbs. Fry fillets in hot oil turning them until golden brown. Enjoy!

Recipe Courtesy: Loretta Cicerrella

Marblehead Lighthouse
Marblehead Peninsula, Ohio, Lake Erie

U.S. Coast Guard Collection

Marblehead Lighthouse is the oldest continuously operating lighthouse on the Great Lakes. Perched at the end of the Marblehead Peninsula, it marks the northern end of Sandusky Bay. The area is rich with history. Johnson's Island to the south was the home of a prison camp for Confederate soldiers. Kellys Island to the north was the site of a limestone quarry that provided stone for many Great Lakes lighthouse towers. To the northeast are South Bass Island and Perry's Victory and International Peace Memorial. The victory of Commodore Oliver Hazard Perry's small fleet over the powerful British squadron on Lake Erie on September 10, 1813 was a critical turning point in the War of 1812 and Perry literally saved the Great Lakes and entire Midwest for the United States.

The light at Marblehead was built in 1821. The original 50-foot stone tower was increased by 15 feet in 1897. It was converted to electricity in 1923 and automated in 1946. The first keeper was Benajah Wolcott, a Revolutionary War veteran. When he died of cholera his wife Rachel followed as keeper, making her the first female keeper on the Great Lakes.

Today the lighthouse is a maritime museum and a great addition to the story of our Great Lakes.

Oliver Hazard Perry Wedding Plum Cake–Historic

Perry described the cake as, *"Four pounds of flour, four pounds of currants, four pounds of butter, four pounds of sugar, four pounds of citron, one half ounce mace, one half pint of brandy, forty eggs, will make a devilish good wedding cake such as I had."*

Equipment
5 large bowls or kettles for beating, mixing, etc.
3 large pans, 3 1-inch pans, 1 6-inch pan for baking
2 ovens

Line pan bottoms with parchment paper, butter well. Preheat oven to 275 degrees.
Combine in first large bowl:
1 pint cream sherry or brandy
4 pounds currants (raisins may be substituted)
4 pounds citron (may use 1/2 pound citron, 1 pound mixed fruit)
1/2 pound chopped pecans or walnuts
2 pounds candied cherries, chopped
Soak fruit in liqueur in first bowl.

Second and third bowls:
Separate the 40 eggs set aside egg whites in second bowl.
Beat the egg yokes in third bowl for 3 minutes with electric mixer or whisk and set aside.

Cream in fourth bowl:
4 pounds butter (1/2 butter flavored Crisco may be used)

2 pounds of white sugar
2 pounds of light brown sugar
Cream well and add to egg yokes in the third bowl.

Combine in fourth bowl (used in creaming above)
4 pounds of all-purpose flour
3 tablespoons of all spice
4 teaspoons of mace
3 tablespoons of cinnamon
2 teaspoons of nutmeg
1 teaspoon of baking soda

Egg whites:
Beat until medium stiff with 1 teaspoon of salt.

Combine:
Flour and egg yoke mixture alternately with fruit mix.
Fold in egg whites–best to use hands for this step.

Fill pans:
To about 2/3 full.
Bake 1-1/2 to 2 hours. Check for doneness. Cool in pans, turn out and sprinkle with brandy or cream sherry. Wrap in plastic wrap and refrigerate overnight.

Frosting:
1 can of a standard butter cream frosting or 7 minute frosting could be used.

Recipe Courtesy: Lake Erie Islands Historical Society

Michigan City Lighthouse
Michigan City, Indiana, Lake Michigan

Author's Collection

As the importance of the harbor at Michigan City grew, so did the need for a light to guide ships into the harbor. At first a simple lantern hung on a pole was adequate. By 1834 appropriations were secured for an actual lighthouse. Three years later a story and a half lighthouse with projecting 40-foot high stone tower was finished and ready for use.

When shipping continued to grow a new more powerful light was erected in 1858. The three-floored building was made of a Joliet stone foundation and Milwaukee brick superstructure. A lens cupola extended through the north end of the roof. The fifth order Fresnel provided a beam visible for fifteen miles.

Michigan City Light was a rarity in that women keepers were often appointed to it. From 1844-1853, Mrs. Harriet Tower was the keeper and her sister Miss Abigail Coit, acted as her assistant.

The keeper most identified with Michigan City Light was Harriet E. Colfax, appointed on March 19, 1861. She held the keeper's position for 33 years, retiring in 1904 at age 80. During this period of lighthouse history keepers were appointed by political connections and Harriet used hers to secure the position. Since her first cousin was Schuyler Colfax, speaker of the House of Representatives and later Vice President for U.S. Grant, her connections were impeccable.

Nothing in Harriet's background prepared her for the job. Normally a woman appointed as a lightkeeper had been a keeper's wife or daughter. She would have already known the job before being appointed. Harriet, who had no prior lighthouse experience, was a music and voice teacher. In spite of this handicap, she learned quickly and was soon recognized as a dependable and efficient keeper.

On November 20, 1871 a light was added to the east breakwater pier. In time the shore light was discontinued. Today the original lighthouse is a museum and the old fifth order Fresnel is a popular exhibit.

Indiana Lamb Chops—Contemporary

12 loin or rib lamb chops

2 tablespoons fresh chopped oregano or 2 teaspoons dried oregano

Salt and pepper to taste

4 tablespoons olive oil

3 small zucchini, sliced

2 medium red onions, sliced

1 clove garlic, minced

3 medium tomatoes cut in wedges

3/4 teaspoon dried basil or 1 tablespoon chopped fresh basil

Linguine pasta, cooked and drained

Lamb has long been a staple of the American diet. Whether a gourmet or weekend chef, lamb is a natural choice for simple or creative meals.

Sprinkle lamb chops with oregano, salt and pepper. Brown chops in 3 tablespoons olive oil, 4-5 minutes each side. Remove and keep hot. Heat remaining tablespoon oil. Sauté zucchini, onion and garlic until tender. Add tomatoes and basil; cook 2 minutes more. Toss together with pasta. Arrange on platter with lamb chops. Makes 6 servings.

Recipe Courtesy: Hoosier KitcheNet, http://www.ind.com/KitcheNet

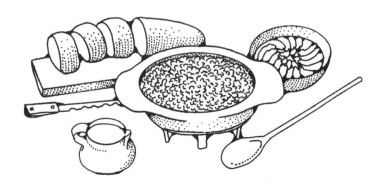

Grosse Point Lighthouse
Evanston, Illinois, Lake Michigan

U.S. Coast Guard Collection

Grosse Point Light is one of only five lights on the Great Lakes to be equipped with a second order Fresnel lens. It is the only one still using its lens. Located just north of Chicago, it was an important aid to guide shipping past an extensive series of offshore shoals.

The light was built in 1873 and first illuminated for the start of navigation on March 1, 1874. It was designed by Orlando M. Poe, famous for being General William Tecumseh Sherman's engineer during the Civil War. Grosse Point Light has a higher level of detail than most Great Lakes lights. Corbels grace the top of the brickwork on the 113-foot tower that support the galley. The area above the windows also has unusual accent work.

A duplex keeper's quarters provided living accommodations for the keeper and his assistant. The light only operated for 67 years, a very short span for a major second order light.

During World War II, the lighthouse was the site for secret testing of infrared devices intended to improve radar capability. Scientists from nearby Northwestern University were deeply involved in the research.

The light was electrified in 1923, automated in 1935 and decommissioned in 1941. A series of offshore buoys made the old light superfluous. Good lights are hard to keep down however and in 1946 it was reactivated as a private aid to navigation. The old Fresnel, still in the tower, again sent it's powerful beams out over the backwaters of Lake Michigan. Today the lighthouse is the only maritime museum in the Chicago area.

Thick As Fog Split Pea Soup With Ham-Historic

2 smoked ham hocks (or left over bone with meat from a whole smoked ham)

8 cups of chicken stock

1 1/2 cups split peas (if possible, use the split peas that have been prepared for use in soup)

2 tablespoons butter

1 medium Vidalia (sweet) onion coarsely chopped

1 large carrot peeled and coarsely chopped

The Great Lakes have always experienced an unusual amount of fog and this recipe by Don Terras, resident director of the Grosse Point Lighthouse National Landmark, would have helped many a lighthouse keeper maintain their stamina while firing the old steam boilers that operated the fog signals.

Melt the butter in a 5-quart soup pot and sauté the coarsely chopped onion and carrot until they are soft but not overdone. Add the ham hocks, split peas and 8 cups of chicken stock. Bring to a boil, reduce the heat and simmer for 1 hour. Then remove from heat and take out the ham hocks or ham bone to cool.

Puree the soup in a blender or mash the mixture and whisk vigorously until the desired consistency (as the lightkeepers of old do).

Remove the meat from the ham hocks or ham bone and discard the skin, fat and bone. Pick the meat apart with your fingers into bite sized pieces and add to the soup. Stir and heat through for a 1/2 hour.

Serve in large bowls with lightly seasoned croutons, a garnish of parsley and a twist of fresh ground pepper. Garlic bread and a salad make a nice accompaniment for dinner. Serves 4 for dinner or 6 for lunch.

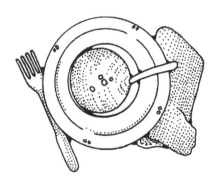

Recipe Courtesy: Don Terras, Resident Director, Grosse Point Lighthouse National Landmark, Grosse Point, Illinois.

Pilot Island Lighthouse
Pilot Island, Wisconsin, Lake Michigan

U.S. Coast Guard Collection

The old keepers or their families never considered being assigned to Pilot Island Lighthouse desirable. The island stands squarely between Detroit Island to the northeast and the rugged west shore of Wisconsin's Door Peninsula to the southwest. The narrow channel that cuts just to the south, named "Porte des Morts" or "Deaths Door Passage" by the early French voyageurs, was a notorious ship trap. As dangerous as it was short, it is still the quickest way from Lake Michigan to Green Bay. Pilot Island received its name from it's relationship to the notorious passage.

The first lighthouse was erected in 1850 and extensively remodeled in 1858. The final result was a two-story brick structure with a short tower projecting through the roof. A fog bell was added in 1862 because of the frequent fogs common to the area.

A visitor in 1890 described the island as, "…a little island of three and a quarter acres of rock and boulders on which there is an imported croquet ground, a few ornamental trees, a strawberry patch, two fog sirens, a lighthouse, a frame barn, a boat house and some blue, bell-shaped flowers and golden-rods that grow out of the niches in the rock."

One historian claimed the only thing that broke the monotony was the frequent shipwrecks. In the fall of 1872 the keeper reported eight schooners stranded or wrecked in the passage in a single week. The prior year a hundred ships were lost or damaged running through the "Door." A single storm on October 30, 1880 wrecked an estimated 30 ships.

Keeper Victor E. Rohn had been an officer during the Civil War. After spending a couple of years on the island he noted in his log for July 4, 1874, "Independence Day came in fine after a heavy southeast gale. This island affords about as much independence and liberty as Libby Prison, with the difference in guards in favor of this place and with the chance for outside communications in favor of the other."

The light was automated in 1962. Today a modern 300 mm optic is used instead of the old Fresnel.

Door County Fish Boil-Historic

16 chunks of whitefish (2 inch slices)

16 small red potatoes (ends cut off)

16 small onions, (peeled)

1/2 pound salt

2 gallons water

Fish boils are an important part of the local cultural heritage. Always popular with tourists, they are best done outside over an open fire pit by an experienced "boil master."

Add 1/4 pound of salt to water and bring to a boil. Add potatoes and boil for 12 minutes. Add onions and boil for 4 minutes longer. Add fish and 1/4 pound of salt. Boil for 10 minutes and drain into colander. Serve with melted butter, lemon and coleslaw.

Author's Note: Although purists maintain the whitefish must be chunks, my preference is to use fillets which eliminates the bone from the final dish.

Recipe Courtesy: Tom Lyons, Marketing Director, Door County Chamber of Commerce

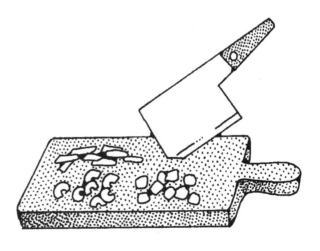

Sand Island Lighthouse
Sand Island, Wisconsin, Lake Superior

Author's Collection

There are seven lighthouses in Wisconsin's Lake Superior Apostle Islands. Some historians consider them to be the best collection of lighthouses in the United States. One of the most colorful of the lights is the one on Sand Island. Built in 1882, the story and a half brownstone structure with it's fourth order Fresnel lens was a vital guide for shipping working through the bewildering array of islands and reefs. It's Norman Gothic style is similar to several other Lake Superior lights, including Eagle Harbor and Passage Island.

Sand Island Light bore silent witness to two tragic shipwrecks. On September 12, 1885 keeper Charles Lederle saw the large steamer *Prussia* on fire about ten miles off shore. Although a strong southeast wind was blowing, he rowed out alone in the station boat to help in anyway he could. Several miles out he met some of the crew, including the captain, rowing to shore in the lifeboat. The master told him the rest of the crew were in the yawl and rapidly being blown out into the lake. Lederle continued on, caught up with the yawl and brought both boats safely back to the lighthouse.

The second disaster happened during a roaring north storm on September 2, 1905 when the big steel steamer *Servona* struck Sand Island Shoal, a mile and a half northeast of the light and quickly broke in two. The 17 men and women on the stern reached shore in the vessel's two lifeboats. The seven men trapped on the bow without a lifeboat hurriedly made a raft and tried to reach Sand Island. Keeper Emmanuel Luick watched helplessly as the makeshift raft was torn apart by the waves and the men drowned. The storm was too fierce for Luick to launch his own boat.

Sand Island Light was automated in 1933 and is currently part of the Apostle Islands National Lakeshore.

Lemon Meringue Pie With Big Wild Blueberries–Historic

1 9-inch baking shell

Pie:

1-1/2 cups sugar

1-1/3 tablespoon cornstarch

3 egg yolks, slightly beaten

1-1/2 cups water

3 tablespoons butter

2 teaspoons lemon peel

1/2 cup lemon juice

1/3 cup big wild blueberries

Meringue:

3 egg whites

1/4 teaspoon cream of tarter

6 tablespoons sugar

1/2 teaspoon vanilla

This wonderful recipe is provided by Lois Spangle, the daughter of Alphonse and Lorna G. Gustafson. Alphonse was the keeper on nearby Long Island from 1938-1946. Lois has many special memories of growing up as a lighthouse keeper's daughter, one of them being picking the biggest, tastiest wild blueberries ever. This recipe is her favorite. As a child she remembers making it for the carpenters who built the new keeper's dwelling at the LaPointe lighthouse on Long Island.

Heat oven to 400 degrees.

Lemon Pie–Stir together sugar and cornstarch in medium saucepan. Blend egg yolks and water, gradually stirring into cornstarch/sugar mixture. Cook over medium heat, stirring constantly, until mixture thickens and boils. Boil and stir for one minute. Remove from heat, stir in butter, lemon peel and lemon juice. Immediately pour mixture into the baked pie shell, along with the big blueberries.

Meringue–Beat egg whites and cream of tarter until white and foamy. Beat in sugar one tablespoon at a time. Continue beating until stiff and glossy. Beat in vanilla. Heap meringue onto hot filling and bake about 10 minutes, watching carefully. Cool completely and enjoy.

Recipe Courtesy: Lois Spangle

The Atlantic Ocean

Cape Elizabeth Lighthouse
Cape Elizabeth, Maine

National Archives

The twin towers of Cape Elizabeth Light are perhaps best known for one of its keepers, Marcus Hanna. Receiving a medal for heroism is very rare but Marcus won two; the Congressional Medal of Honor and the Gold Life-Saving Medal. He won the Medal of Honor during the Civil War when as a member of a Massachusetts Volunteer Infantry Regiment he risked his life braving fierce enemy fire to provide drinking water to his comrades during the Battle of Port Hudson in 1863.

Marcus was the keeper at Cape Elizabeth on January 28, 1885 when the schooner *Australia* smashed into the rocks near the light during a roaring northeaster. His courageous efforts at saving people aboard the wreck resulted in the award of Gold Life-Saving Medal. In recognition of Marcus' rare achievements, the Coast Guard named one of the new Keeper Class buoy tenders *Marcus Hanna* in his honor.

The Cape Elizabeth twin towers are located outside of Portland, Maine and mark the southern bank of the tricky channel into the harbor. The original towers were built in 1828. Since they were cheaply constructed of rubble, they were torn down in 1873 and replaced with two cast iron towers 300 yards apart. The old tower is pictured.

Captain Brigg's Blueberry Lattice Pie–Contemporary

3-1/2 cups blueberries

1/4 cup tapioca

3/4 cup granulated sugar

2 tablespoons butter at room temperature

Pie dough

1 tablespoon sugar mixed with a dash of cinnamon

Pie Dough:

1 cup sweet unsalted butter (2 sticks at room temperature)

1/2 teaspoon salt

3 cups flour

3 tablespoons cold water

Preheat oven to 450 degrees.

Combine blueberries, tapioca, 3/4 cup sugar and butter. Stir together and mush up some berries so mixture is juicy. Do not try to mix thoroughly; there will be chunks of butter in the mixture.

To make dough: combine butter, salt and flour. Cut flour into butter. Rub mixture through fingers until of cornmeal consistency. Add water, turning mixture so it comes together in a ball. If mixture does not stick together, work in an extra tablespoon or two of cold water and chill.

Divide chilled dough into 2 portions, one slightly larger than the other. Roll larger one on floured surface into 12-inch circle. Place rolled dough on 9-inch pie plate. Dough should be about 1/2 inch longer than top of plate. Pour in berry mixture.

Roll out second portion of dough. Cut it into 10 one-inch strips. Place 5 strips across pie in one direction. Weave in second set of strips. Fold bottom layer over top of lattice edges. Crimp. Sprinkle cinnamon sugar over top. Bake on bottom rack for 10 minutes; reduce oven temperatures to 350 degrees and bake 50 minutes longer.

Recipe Courtesy: Captain Briggs House Bed and Breakfast, 4 Maple Avenue, Freeport, Maine 04032, http://www.bnblist.com/me/briggs/

Isle Au Haut Lighthouse
Isle Au Haut, Maine

U.S. Coast Guard Collection

The story of Isle Au Haut Light should really start with, "once upon a time." It has that kind of fairy tale quality to it.

"Once upon a time," there were approximately 800 people living on the small island, including a couple of dozen sea captains. Today there is only 50 or so year round residents with an influx during the short summer season.

"Once upon a time," French explorer Samuel de Champlain discovered the island at the eastern end of Penobscot Bay and gave it it's name, which translates as "High Island," a reference to the elevation compared to surrounding islands.

"Once upon a time," every telephone on the island was a crank style. In fact, Isle Au Haut was reportedly the last community in the entire country to use the archaic instruments!

"Once upon a time," the local waters of eastern Penobscot Bay were very rich fishing grounds. Isle Au Haut was the nearest sheltered harbor with a good holding ground for the boats to run into when sudden storms boiled in from the northeast. To meet the needs of the fishermen for a guiding light and fog bell, the Lighthouse Board established the present light in 1907. The 40-foot brick tower rests firmly on a granite foundation just off the island. A long wooden walkway connects the light with the two-story keeper's house. The light was automated in 1934.

"Once upon a time," in 1986 to be exact, the property, less the lighthouse, was purchased and converted into a wonderful bed and breakfast called the Keeper's House. Gourmet meals are the order of the day at the Keeper's House to the certain delight of the guests. The light tower was restored in 1999 and is still an active aid to navigation. A solar powered optic is now in the tower and the original fourth order Fresnel is on display in the Shore Village Museum in Rockland, Maine.

Ida's Sea Clam Pie–Contemporary

1 double pie shell

10-12 sea clams (hen or surf clams), ground or chopped (save juice when opening clams)

1 large piece salt pork, sliced fine

1 medium onion, chopped

1/2 teaspoon pepper

2 tablespoons butter

2 tablespoons lemon juice

The sea clam is also known as surf clam, bar clam, hen clam or skimmer. It is the largest clam reaching 5-9 inches in size. They are found on exposed sand flats at low tide and are gathered with a rake or by hand.

Fry chopped onion in salt pork until tender. Remove salt pork. Add clams and 1/2 cup clam juice. Let simmer on low heat until tender, about 10 minutes. Sprinkle with pepper and lemon juice. Put mixture in pie shell. Add a small amount of clam juice. Reserve remaining juice for gravy. Pat butter on top of clams. Add top crust. Bake 10 minutes at 450 degrees and 30 minutes at 350 degrees. While pie is baking, prepare gravy. Serve pie hot out of the oven topped with gravy.

Gravy: Make a roux with 2 tablespoons of butter whisked into 2 tablespoons of flour. Add clam juice and allow to thicken over heat. Add a bit of milk.

Recipe Courtesy: *Island Lighthouse Inn, A Chronicle,* Jeffrey Burke, The Pilgrim Press, Cleveland, Ohio, 1997; The Keeper's House, PO Box 26, Isle au Haut, Maine, 04645

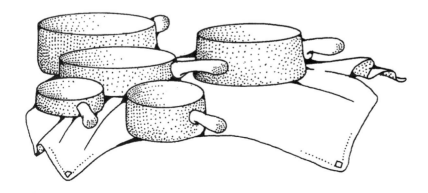

Matinicus Rock Lighthouse
Matinicus Rock, Maine

U.S. Coast Guard Collection

Matinicus Rock is 22 miles off Penobscot Maine. By any standard, it is a forsaken place, just rock, sky and the constant pounding of the ocean. One bored keeper measured it at a mere 2,350 feet by 565 feet. An early report described it as having, "…neither trees and hardly a blade of grass." It is rock and nothing more. During storms waves can sweep completely over the lonely isle. It is the most isolated light along the Maine coast.

The first lighthouse was built on Matinicus Rock in 1826. It was not strongly built, being only a wood house with a wood tower at each end, thus showing distinctive twin lights. A new structure was built in 1848 but didn't last and the present cut stone towers were constructed nine years later. The towers were 80 feet apart with a stone keeper's house in between, and third order Fresnel lenses in the lantern rooms.

Matinicus Rock is best known for the exploits of Abbie Burgess. In January 1856 her keeper father Samuel rowed to the mainland for provisions. The supply boat had not arrived and it was important that a stock of food be secured before the worst of winter arrived. Before he left, Sam told 16-year old Abbie to keep the light burning until he returned in a day or so. A short time after he left the wind veered northeast and began to blow hard.

The storm increased in violence. For three long days the wind and sea grew more fearsome. On the morning of the fourth day a wave smashed into the house. Fearing it would collapse, Abbie moved her invalid mother and young brother to shelter in the north light tower. Throughout the raging storm, Abbie made her way from tower to tower to keep the lights burning. Abbie and her family nearly ran out of food, at one point, down to a day's ration of an egg and a cup of cornmeal each. She kept up her frantic pace of caring for both family and lights until the storm died and her father returned.

After the presidential election of 1860, Sam Burgess was replaced by John Grant whose son Isaac was appointed as the assistant keeper. Since Abbie was familiar with the routine of running the lights, she stayed on to teach the Grants the intricacies of the job. Isaac was so impressed with the 22-year-old Abbie that he proposed marriage. The following year they were wed and she officially became the second assistant keeper. In 1875 Isaac was transferred to White Head Light, 20 miles distant.

When the use of multiple lights to provide unique characteristics stopped in 1924, one of the towers was deactivated. The remaining light was automated in 1983.

The exploits of brave Abbie Burgess live on. In 1997 the Coast Guard accepted delivery of the *Abbie Burgess*, WLM 553, a 175-foot Keeper Class buoy tender built by Marinette Marine Corporation in Marinette, Wisconsin. It is a fine tribute to a courageous lightkeeper.

Maine Lobster Sauté~Contemporary

1 teaspoon olive oil

1 teaspoon each chopped garlic and shallot

1 teaspoon oregano

8 ounces mushrooms

1/2 cup sliced onions

1/2 cup sliced red peppers

8 ounces diced plum type tomatoes

Splash of Chablis

1/2 teaspoon basil

1/2 teaspoon thyme

1/4 cup parsley

1/2 pound cooked Maine lobster

Salt and pepper to taste

Maine Lobster can be simple and elegant when served with wine or champagne. The centerpiece of a summer cookout. This recipe is certainly worthy of note.

In a sauté pan over medium heat start the first 3 ingredients. When starting to sweat, increase heat to high and add the veggies. Sauté quickly and add the wine (about 2 minutes). Add the herbs and lobster, stir then cover and steam, sauté for a minute or so until veggies are done the way you like them (aldente) …low-fat yet tasty, serve over rice or tossed with fettuccine…BON APPETIT!

Recipe Courtesy: Hattie's Chowder House, 103 Water Street, Hallowell, Maine, 04347, http://www.hattieslobsterstew.com

Mount Desert Rock Lighthouse
Bar Harbor, Maine

National Archives

One of the most colorful lights on the Maine coast is at Mount Desert Rock off Bar Harbor. The small island is barely 17 feet above sea level and is constantly lashed by waves. During one storm a 75-ton boulder was moved 60 feet! The nearest harbor is at Mount Desert Island, 20 miles distant. The light is the most outlying beacon on the Maine coast. French explorer Samuel de Champlain named both Island and Rock in 1604.

The first light was erected in 1830. It was a small wood tower attached to a wood keeper's house and used eight lamps and reflectors. Doubtless the poorly built structure suffered heavily from wave and wind before being replaced in 1847 by a 58-foot granite tower. The wood house remained in use until 1876 when it was torn down and new quarters built. The present house was built in 1893. A third order Fresnel lens was added in 1858, vastly increasing the lights range and efficiency.

The rock was the scene of numerous shipwrecks. Particularly noteworthy is the wreck of the tug *Astral* in December 1902. It smashed into the ledge at the northeast point in the midst of a terrific gale. The waves were breaking so high it looked certain that all of the men aboard would perish. When the tide dropped however, the keeper and his assistants were able to get a rope to the ship and all of the crew except for one already dead, were able to climb to safety. The men spent six days on the rock waiting until the weather moderated enough to allow them to leave.

For a time there was a tradition that each spring the families would bring enough soil to the rock to be able to grow a flower garden. The sight of bright and cheery flowers was an important morale booster for the people on the desolate and forbidding rock pile. The growing season was short however, and when the fall gales came the waves washed the gardens away.

In the 1970s the Coast Guard removed the lens, substituting an aero beacon. Today the station is owned by the College of the Atlantic and used as a whale research facility. Humpback and finback whale are common to the area.

Jasper's Baked Stuffed Maine Lobster–Contemporary

1 live lobster, about 1 to 1-1/2 pounds

3 ounces (about 1/2 cup) Ritz cracker crumbs

1 tablespoon Parmesan cheese, grated

1/2 stick butter, melted

1 ounce scallops

2 ounces shrimp

3 ounces haddock

Maine lobsters are caught the old fashioned way–hauling one trap at a time from the sea floor. It is a very labor intensive process.

Recipe is for stuffing 1 lobster. Multiply ingredients by number of lobsters.

Preheat oven to 450 degrees F.

Split live lobsters with a sharp, pointed knife from head to tail. Open flat and remove intestinal vein, stomach and tomalley. If desired save tomalley to add to stuffing. Crack claws, remove meat and cut into pieces.

Moisten crumbs with butter and egg. Then add Parmesan cheese, tomalley and fresh raw seafood. Spread stuffing mixture generously in cavity and split tail.

Place on cookie sheet and bake for 30 minutes.

Recipe Courtesy: Fred Graham, Jasper's Restaurant and Motel, Route 1, 200 High Street, Ellsworth, Maine, 04605

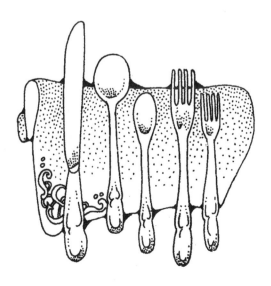

93

Portland Head Lighthouse
Cape Elizabeth, Maine

Author's Collection

Following the Revolutionary War, the few existing lighthouses were still under the providence of the various states and it seemed likely they would continue to be a state responsibility. The construction of Portland Head Lighthouse was started by the Massachusetts legislature in 1787 with an appropriation of $750. At the time the present state of Maine was part of Massachusetts. When the Federal government took over the lights in 1790, Congress provided $1,500 to finish the job.

Completed on January 10, 1791, the tower would eventually reach 72 feet tall. As originally built, it was only 58 feet high. When it became apparent this was too low to be seen over an adjacent headland, an extra 14 feet were added. A chandelier of 16 lamps and reflectors provided the illumination. A small one-story keeper's house was also built. A new set of quarters would be erected in 1891.

As with many early lighthouses there were problems with construction quality. Damp stone and rotting timber needed constant attention. There were also complaints about the quality of the light. Vessel captains criticized it as too dim and the keeper responded the lamps sooted up quickly due to poor ventilation.

In 1864 a fourth order Fresnel was installed replacing the ineffective lamp and reflector system. A year later the tower was raised 20 feet to increase visibility and in 1866 the small lens was replaced with a larger second order Fresnel.

On Christmas Eve 1886, the three-masted bark *Annie C. Maguire* ran hard onto the rock ledge at Portland Head. As the night was clear and the crew later admitted having seen the light, the accident was inexplicable. Keeper Joshua Strout, his son, wife and several volunteers responded to the wreck by rigging a ladder as a gangplank between the ship and shore rocks to allow the crew to reach safety.

In 1989 the Coast Guard decommissioned the light and the property was later transferred to the town of Cape Elizabeth. The light however is still an active aid. Portland Head Light Museum presently occupies the old 1891 keeper's quarters.

Shrimp Scampi–Contemporary

1/4 cup sun dried tomato pesto

1 pound shrimp

2 teaspoons chopped garlic

1/4 teaspoon salt

1/8 teaspoon pepper

2 teaspoons lemon juice

2 cups hot cooked rice

Shrimp are always a great seafood treat. No matter how they are prepared, they always "hit the spot!"

Cook pesto in skillet while stirring over medium heat 2 minutes or until fragrant. Add shrimp and chopped garlic. Cook 5 minutes stirring constantly or until shrimp turns opaque. Add salt, pepper and lemon juice. Blend and serve over rice.

Recipe Courtesy: The Inn at St. John, 939 Congress Street, Portland, Maine, 800-636-9127, www.innatstjohn.com

Ram Island Lighthouse
Booth Bay Harbor, Maine

U.S. Coast Guard Collection

Ram Island Light marks the dangerous Fisherman's Passage into Booth Bay Harbor. The area has seen many shipwrecks. Although the present lighthouse dates only from 1883, lights were exhibited on the island well before then. In the mid 1800s fishermen hung lanterns on the island to aid their fellows in slipping past the dangerous rock ledges. The duty was passed on from man to man as needed. In spite of the lanterns, ships wrecked in the area with accompanying loss of life.

There are stories of ghosts on the island too. One captain reported that while entering the harbor in a snowstorm, an eerie foghorn warned him away from the shoals, although he knew there was no foghorn on the island. Another boat captain was headed for the rocks when a spectral woman in white, waving a burning torch, suddenly appeared and warned the craft away! A captain claimed he was alerted to impending disaster on the ledges when he sighted a burning ship on the island. He turned away in time. Visiting the island later, he found no evidence of a fire, not even a charred piece of wood.

The government finally erected a light in 1883. The brick tower is built on a granite foundation and connected to shore by a wood catwalk. A Victorian keeper's house was located on shore. A fog bell was added in 1897. Life on the island seems to have an unusual effect on keepers and their wives. It is alleged one keeper and his wife had 15 children born on the island and another keeper and his wife nearly as many.

Ram Island Light was automated in 1965 and the keeper's house removed. The fourth order Fresnel lens was stolen in 1975 but eventually recovered.

Maine Lobster Stew–Contemporary

1/4 cup chopped scallion

1/2 cup butter

3 pinches thyme

1/4 cup dry sherry

Salt and pepper

3 cups medium cream

1 pound fresh cooked lobster meat

Pilot crackers

Lobster of course is an important part of the historic diet for coastal residents of the northeast United States and there are many wonderful ways to prepare it.

In skillet sauté scallions. Butter and thyme for 4 minutes. Add sherry, salt and pepper. Bring to a boil for 1 minute. Add cream and lobster and bring to a near boil. Serve hot with pilot crackers.

Recipe Courtesy: The Inn at St. John, 939 Congress Street, Portland, Maine, 800-636-9127, www.innatstjohn.com

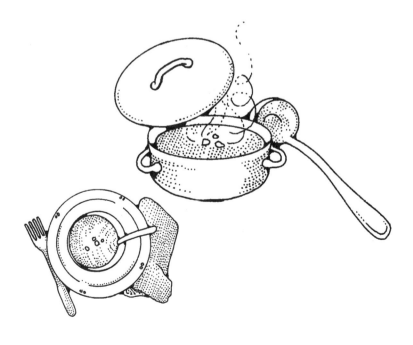

Spring Point Ledge Lighthouse
South Portland, Maine

Author's Collection

In 1891 several steamship companies lobbied the government for the construction of a light at Spring Point Ledge. The rock outcrop is a treacherous shoal on the west side of the main shipping channel into Portland Harbor. During the previous year the companies carried over 500,000 passengers through the passage so they certainly had a viable interest in having a safe channel marked.

The light is a very typical "sparkplug" style. Although instead of being built of cast iron, the tower is brick. Congress originally appropriated $20,000 for the project but various delays including concerns about the quality of the cement increased the final cost to $45,000. The fifth order Fresnel was illuminated on May 24, 1897. The tower was self-contained in that everything needed for operating the light, quarters for two keepers, oil storage, etc., were in the structure.

Spring Point Ledge Light was also a stag station. Only male keepers were assigned there. Sleeping at the light was difficult for new keepers. Since the fog bell was mounted on the side of the tower. Powered by a clockwork mechanism, it rang twice every 12 seconds, which certainly could be disturbing to anyone nearby.

The light was electrified and automated in 1934. A 900-foot long granite breakwater was extended from shore to the light in 1951. The light is now part of the Portland Harbor Museum and will continue to be an important part of local maritime history.

Maine Blueberry Cake–Contemporary

1 cup sugar

1/2 cup oil

1/3 cup milk

1 teaspoon vanilla

2 eggs, separated

1-1/2 cups flour

1/4 teaspoon salt

1 teaspoon baking powder

1 cup Maine frozen blueberries

The blueberry is a native American species. Ninety percent of the world's blueberry supply is grown in North America. Early settlers used them in food and medicines. They ate them fresh off the bush and added them to soups, stews, beer and other foods.

In mixer blend sugar, oil, milk, vanilla and egg yolks. Mix together flour, salt and baking powder and add to mixture. Flour frozen blueberries and add to cake mixture. Fold in lightly. Grease and flour 9 x 9 cake pan. Bake at 375º for 30 minutes. Serve plain, with whipped cream or ice cream.

Recipe Courtesy: The Inn at St. John, 939 Congress Street, Portland, Maine, 800-636-9127, www.innatstjohn.com/

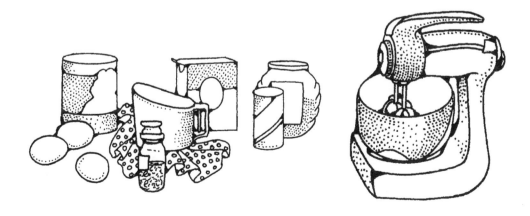

West Quoddy Head Lighthouse Lubec, Maine

West Quoddy Head Light is unique in that it is located on the most eastern point of the U.S. mainland. The coast is rock bound and most forbidding. The need for the light was identified in 1806 when a group of citizens selected West Quoddy Head as the best place for a beacon to assist mariners running into the west entrance to Quoddy Roads between the mainland and Campobello Island. Two years later a rubble tower was constructed by order of President Thomas Jefferson.

The soil at the light was so thin; it was incapable of supporting even a small vegetable garden, which was a significant problem for the early keepers. In compensation, the first keeper received a raise of $50 annually to purchase food he normally would have grown.

The fog at West Quoddy Head was legendary. To help warn ships away from dangerous Sail Rocks just off the light, the keeper was issued a small cannon. When the fog rolled in, he was expected to blast away, sending a loud retort out into the gray mist. The cannon proved generally ineffective and very costly, so in 1820 he was given one of the first fog bells provided to any lighthouse. The bell had to be used so often that in 1827 the keeper was granted an increase of $60 annually for the extra work.

The light was rebuilt in 1858 resulting in the present 49-foot tower. At the same time the old lamps and reflectors were exchanged for a modern third order Fresnel lens. The following year a new keeper's house was built.

West Quoddy Head Light was a difficult place to raise a family. In the 1920s the keeper's children had a walk of about two miles to get to school. Combined with the frequent fog and resulting bell ringing, it also must have been difficult to concentrate on homework.

The grounds of the West Quoddy Head Light are part of Quoddy Head State Park and the lighthouse proper is now owned by the State of Maine. The light is still an active aid to navigation.

Lobster Waffles–Contemporary

Waffles:

1/2 pound cooked lobster meat

3 cups waffle mix

1/2 cup lemon butter, recipe below

Lemon Butter:

1/2 cup butter or margarine

1 teaspoon lemon juice

1/4 teaspoon grated lemon rind

This recipe certainly shows another very innovative and imaginative way lobster can be used in new and exciting ways!

Chop lobster meat. Prepare waffle mix as directed. Add lobster meat. Bake in a hot waffle iron until brown. Serve with lemon butter.

Lemon Butter: Whip butter. Slowly add lemon juice and rind.

Recipe Courtesy: U.S. Fish and Wildlife Service and Maine Lobster Promotion Council, http://www.mainelobsterpromo.com

Bishop And Clerks Lighthouse
Nantucket Sound, Massachusetts

U.S. Coast Guard Collection

Bishop and Clerks Light was built in 1858 to designate the hazardous pile of rocks called Bishop and Clerks in Nantucket Sound off Hyannis on Cape Cod. Originally a day marker was placed on the rocks and later a lightship was moored in the area. After time however, the Lighthouse Board decided a true lighthouse was needed. Constructing the light was difficult because of it's remote location. Some people even compared it to the project at Minot's Ledge. The final product was a 65-foot high granite tower topped with a fourth order Fresnel lens. After becoming operational, the light at nearby Point Gammons was discontinued and the keeper transferred to Bishop and Clerks. Keeper John Peak was nothing if not loyal. He stayed at the light until his retirement in 1886, a remarkable 62 years of lighthouse service. Perhaps Peak liked the remote life. Keepers at Bishop and Clerks spent 20 days at the light, then ten days off. Although the tower had two bedrooms and a kitchen, the facilities were spartan and certainly gave no incentive to spend more time than required trapped in the granite tower.

The light was automated in 1923 and discontinued in 1928. A storm in 1935 shattered the integrity of the structure badly and the continued buffeting by wind and wave during the following years wore away at it constantly. By 1952 the tower was leaning to one side and clearly about to collapse. Rather than repair a discontinued light, the Coast Guard decided to tear it down and on September 11 of that year a well-placed charge of explosives knocked it over into a pile of rubble. Today a small "pipe" tower marks the reef. The old stone tower is but a memory.

Basic Corn Bread–Historic

1 cup yellow cornmeal

1 cup all-purpose flour

3/4 teaspoon baking soda

2 teaspoons baking powder

1-1/2 teaspoons salt

3/4 teaspoon freshly ground black pepper

1 egg, lightly beaten

1-1/2 cups buttermilk

2 tablespoons butter or rendered bacon fat

This recipe makes a great, not-too-sweet bread with a dry texture.

Mix together cornmeal, flour, baking soda, baking powder, salt and pepper. Combine the egg and buttermilk, add them to the dry ingredients and stir to combine. Heat the butter in a 10-inch ovenproof skillet over moderate heat until bubbly. Tilt to coat the pan; pour in the batter. Cook the bread on the stove for about 3 minutes to give it a good crust. Put the skillet in a 375º preheated oven to bake until a toothpick inserted in the center of the bread comes out clean, 20 to 25 minutes. Turn the corn bread out on a rack so it doesn't stick.

Recipe Courtesy: www.maineberries.com

Boston Lighthouse
Little Brewster Island, Massachusetts

National Archives

Boston Light gets all the credit! Many people consider it the most historic lighthouse in America. Historian Edward Rowe Snow called it, "the ideal American Lighthouse." These judgments are only opinions and nothing more. The real facts are a little different.

The first true lighthouse built in America was on Little Brewster Island in Boston Harbor in 1716. This light was completely destroyed in 1776 and not rebuilt until 1783. The oldest standing and still in use lighthouse is at Sandy Hook, New Jersey. It was built in 1764. While Boston Light is certainly a historically significant light, it is regional boosterism to consider it, "the ideal American Light."

The lighthouse was built by the merchants of Boston and financed by the tax of a penny a ton on all vessels entering or leaving the harbor. In July 1775 the British controlled Boston Harbor. In response to a group of Colonial troops burning the wooden part of the tower, the British seized the light and attempted to repair the damage, but the Americans struck again, burning the recently repaired section. When British forces departed Boston on June 13, 1776 they blew up the lighthouse destroying it completely.

The light was reestablished in 1783 when a 75-foot rubble tower was built on the island by order of John Hancock, Governor or Massachusetts. This is the start of the current light.

In 1859 the tower was raised 12 feet and a second order Fresnel lens added. Other improvements through the years included cisterns, new foghorns, keeper's houses, oil houses and docks. All are typical of light station development. Keepers and their families were an ever-changing part of the lights history. In the 1930s there were 16 children on the small island between the keeper and his two assistants.

In order not to provide navigational aid to enemy submarines, the light was extinguished during World War II. In 1948 it was electrified. The original Fresnel remains in the tower.

The Coast Guard decided the old 1859 keeper's building was no longer needed and destroyed it in 1960. The lighthouse was scheduled to be automated in 1989, but after political pressure the Coast Guard delayed it until 1998. A coast guard crew continues to man the other functions of lightkeeping.

Boston Light is certainly one of America's most storied lighthouses, but it is not the most historic.

Boston Baked Beans~Historic

4 cups small white beans

2 small onions

1/2 pound salt pork or fatty bacon

2 teaspoons salt

1/2 teaspoon pepper

2 teaspoons mustard

1 cup dark molasses

What can be more "Boston" than Boston baked beans?

Soak the beans in cold water for 12-24 hours. If not soaked this long, or drier than usual, you may have to simmer them until their skins just start to burst.

After soaking the beans, cut the onions in quarters and add to the bottom of the bean pot with the drained beans. Disperse the salt pork chunks throughout the beans. Mix all of the other ingredients with 2-4 cups of hot water and pour over the beans. Cover the beans with water and put the pot into the coals at the back of the kitchen hearth (or in oven at 250 degrees or so, if a handy hearth isn't available).

Cook 6-8 hours, adding water as needed and occasionally stirring up the beans. For the last hour or so leave the pot uncovered to eliminate excess water.

Recipe Courtesy: The Old Lightkeeper

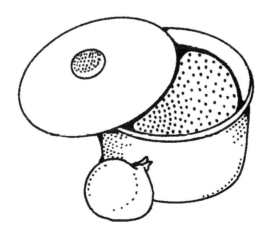

Gay Head Lighthouse
Martha's Vineyard, Massachusetts

U.S. Coast Guard Collection

Gay Head Lighthouse is one of five lights on Martha's Vineyard. It is also the oldest, authorized by Congress in 1789 and completed a year later. An 1852 report claimed it was the ninth most important light in America, due in large part to its critical role of guiding ships into Vineyard Sound from Buzzard's Bay.

The original tower was octagonal in shape. In 1856, the present 51-foot high conical brick tower was finished and a new first order Fresnel lens installed. Sitting on top of a 130-foot high cliff the light has a focal plane of 170 feet. The Fresnel was removed when the light was automated in 1952 and replaced with a DCB-224 aero beacon. The Fresnel is on display at the Martha's Vineyard Historical Museum in Edgartown. The light is still an active aid.

Ebenezer Skiff was the first lightkeeper. With an annual salary of $200. Finding it too low, in 1805 he wrote to the Secretary of the Treasury asking for an increase based on the additional work of cleaning the glass of the lantern room and the long distance he had to haul fresh water. President Jefferson approved an increase of $50. Ten years later he again requested an increase in consideration of a host of factors, including the high price of firewood, distance from freshwater and the cost of hiring a person to watch the light when he was absent on chores. President Madison approved an increase of $50.

Gay Head was the scene of at least one tragic shipwreck. On January 19, 1884 the steamer *City Of Columbus* struck the reef below the light in a storm. Within twenty minutes 100 people drowned. Keeper Horace Pease assembled a crew of local Indians and attempted to reach the wreck in a lifeboat. Their first try failed when the boat overturned in the surf. Undaunted, Pease and his crew tried again, this time reaching the wreck and rescuing many of the victims.

Today the red brick tower with black lantern house stands alone at the edge of the cliff, a silent sentinel to the ever-changing sea.

Gay Head New England Clam Chowder–Contemporary

4 Slices bacon, diced

1-1/2 cups chopped onion

4 cups peeled and cubed potatoes

1-1/2 teaspoons salt

ground black pepper to taste

1-1/2 cups water

2 (6-1/2 ounce) cans minced clams

3 cups half and half cream

3 tablespoons margarine

There must be a thousand good recipes for clam chowder. This one is both reflective of the history of the dish and illustrative of innovative style.

Sauté bacon in large kettle until almost crisp. Add onion, cook 5 minutes. Add cubed potatoes, salt, pepper to taste, 1-1/2 cups water, cook uncovered 15 minutes or until potatoes are fork tender. Meanwhile drain clams, reserving clam liquid. Add clams, 1/2 of the clam liquid, half and half, and butter to the kettle. Mix well and heat about 3 minutes or until heated through. Do not allow to boil. Yield: 8 servings

Recipe Courtesy: Karen Flanders Eddy, Rootsweb-L@rootsweb.com

Great Point Lighthouse
Nantucket Island, Massachusetts

U.S. Coast Guard Collection

The lighthouse at Great Point on Nantucket Island was very important during the early history of America. Nantucket was world famous for their whaling fleet, which in 1775 numbered over 150 ships. In addition there was heavy coasting traffic and an important fishing industry.

In 1770 Nantucket residents petitioned the government for a lighthouse but it was not until 1784 that the General Court of Massachusetts appropriated money for the construction. The result was a simple wooden tower without a keeper's house. The keeper had to ride seven miles on horseback over the dunes to reach the lonely light.

In 1816 the light tower was destroyed by fire. Although there was a suspicion of arson, no official charges were ever made. Two years later a new 60-foot stone tower and keeper's house was in operation. It was equipped with the normal complement of Lewis lamps and reflectors. A third order Fresnel was fitted in 1857. A brick lining was later added to the inside of the tower.

Regardless of the new lens, the area continued to be a magnet for shipwrecks. Between 1863-1890, approximately 43 vessels wrecked near the lighthouse. It is believed many occurred because their captains confused the light with the Cross Rip lightship. The keepers were frequently able to assist shipwreck victims. In 1915 the keeper was recognized with a life-saving medal for saving 14 people and a cat from a wreck.

The light was automated in the 1950s and in 1966 the keeper's house was destroyed by another suspicious fire. Again, nothing was ever proven. By this time, the eroding beach had moved close to the tower and local efforts to convince the Coast Guard to move the tower failed. It was ultimately a case of the Coast Guard being penny wise and pound-foolish. In March 1984 the old tower was destroyed during a storm.

Galvanized by the loss of the historic 1818 tower, local residents lobbied Massachusetts Senator Ted Kennedy, who provided $2 million in Federal money to rebuild the tower further inland. The replica tower was finished in 1986 at a cost of over $1 million. The remainder of the money was used to restore the lights at Cape Poge and Monomoy Point.

Lobster Salad Rolls–Historic

2 cups finely chopped lobster meat

1/2 cup finely chopped celery

Sprinkle of lemon juice

1/2 cup mayonnaise (approximately)

Pinch of curry powder (optional)

Grated Onion (optional)

Salt

Freshly ground black pepper

Softened butter

5 frankfurter rolls

Shredded lettuce

Elsie Grieder, whose husband was a keeper at Great Point Lighthouse, provides this special recipe. She is also a wonderful cook and for a time ran a luncheonette in Gay Head. The secret of the delicious filling is to chop the lobster meat very fine. It was also very important to butter every bit of the frankfurter roll and to grill it very slowly.

Combine lobster meat and celery and sprinkle lightly with lemon juice. Mix slightly, and then add enough mayonnaise to bind mixture and stir well. Add a pinch of curry powder and grated onion to taste, if desired. Add salt and pepper to taste and mix well.

Partially slice frankfurter rolls if necessary, butter the outside surfaces well, heat griddle or heavy skillet and toast rolls slowly on both sides until golden. Put about 2 tablespoons shredded lettuce inside each toasted roll (this makes a bed for the salad) and spoon in about 1/2 cup of the salad on the lettuce, spreading evenly. Keep cool until eaten.

Remember: do not carry unrefrigerated lobster rolls around with you on a hot day. The combination of seafood and mayonnaise is a frequent source of food poisoning.

Recipe Courtesy: Elsie Grieder, Great Point Lighthouse, Nantucket Island

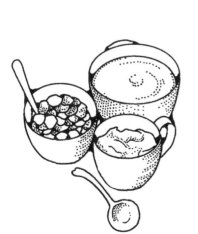

Hospital Point Lighthouse
Beverly, Massachusetts

U.S. Coast Guard Collection

Hospital Point Lighthouse in Beverly, is in an area with an incredibly colorful history. Originally settled in 1626 as Naumkeag, the settlement's name was later changed to Salem. The infamous witchcraft scare of 1692 began and ended in Beverly. When the hysteria was over, 19 women and one man had been executed for practicing witchcraft!

During the Revolution, Beverly was the only town outside of the Boston area in which George Washington established a naval base. Beverly was also a center of privateering. In the latter part of the 18th Century the town became part of the industrial revolution and in the 1890s wealthy Boston families were vacationing in the area. As the result of the many beautiful gardens in the town, it was also called the, "Garden City."

The land where the lighthouse stands was originally used for a smallpox hospital. During the War of 1812, it became a military barracks. In 1849 the building burned down and the land was eventually transferred to the Federal government in 1871 for lighthouse use.

The lighthouse was completed in 1872. It includes a 45-foot high tower and attached two-story keeper's quarters. Major modifications were made in 1947 and 1968. Today it serves as the home for the Commander, First Coast Guard District. The original 3-1/2 order Fresnel is still in use although it was automated in 1947. The lens is unique as it uses a special glass-condensing panel to cause the beam to diminish in intensity if a mariner goes off course entering harbor. In 1927 the light became the front range with the rear located high on a church steeple. Lining up the two lights vertically provides an additional safety feature to keep a true course in the entrance channel.

The rocky locale beneath the light historically has been a lover's lane. It was said, "many a Beverly maid's heart was lost and found on the rocks beneath the faithful light."

Hospital Point Seafood Chowder–Historic

4 potatoes

1 medium onion (or 2 small)

5 2-inch pieces of salted pork (washed)

1-1/2 pound haddock

1/4 tablespoon pepper

1/4 tablespoon salt

milk or half and half

Quarter and slice 4 raw potatoes over 1/2 inch thick. Chop onion very fine. Fry salt pork over medium heat until lightly brown and crisp. Put the potatoes in the bottom of a saucepan and pour onions over potatoes. Lay the fish, in large chunks, over the onions. Pour the salt pork and rendered oil over all. Add cold water, sparingly, to just cover the potatoes. Salt and pepper to taste. Cover loosely and cook over low heat until onions are transparent and potatoes are done. The fish will be well done at this point. Add milk to cover the fish completely. Bring to heat and serve. Yield: 4 servings

Recipe Courtesy: Daniel McPherson, Beverly, Massachusetts

Minot's Ledge Lighthouse
Minot's Ledge, Boston, Massachusetts

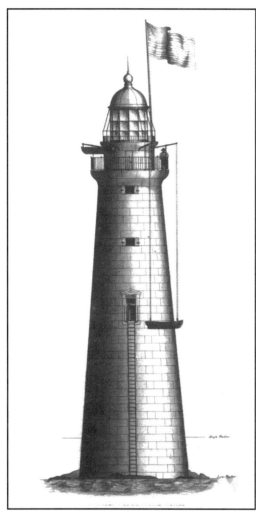

U.S. Coast Guard Collection

Minot's Ledge off Boston has long been a magnet for shipwrecks, the first disaster occurring in 1693. Between 1754-1850, at least 76 vessels plowed into the deadly menace of Cohasset shoals with a loss of an estimated 400 lives.

In 1847 plans were drawn up for a nine-legged iron pile lighthouse. In theory the relatively narrow legs would allow the waves to pass safely beneath without significant force smashing against the structure. It was an extremely difficult build. Only a very small part of the ledge was exposed for two or three hours a day during low tide and then only on calm water days. Construction started in 1848 and on January 1, 1850 the light was illuminated for the first time. The keeper however complained that the lighthouse was not stable and when nothing was done to fix it, he quit. Critical leg cross bracing had been omitted from construction which the builder thought were unneeded. The new keeper and his two assistants didn't like the situation any better, complaining that the cabin room shook like a "…drunken man on a step ladder." On April 11, 1851 the keeper left the light on leave. Five days later the tower collapsed in a storm killing both assistants. It was a devastating loss. Everyone had considered the new tower safe against any storm.

Following the disaster the new Lighthouse Board decided they needed to be very serious about a new lighthouse. Desperate to avoid a repetition of the catastrophe the job of designing and building the new tower was given to the U.S. Army Corps of Engineers. Their carefully prepared plans called for a 114-foot tall granite block tower. Bolstered by a $300,000 Congressional appropriation, they started to work in 1855. The stone blocks were dovetailed to fit together such that they were interlocked into a solid whole. When the light was lit on November 15, 1860 nearby Sictuate Light was discontinued. In celebration of the new light, bonfires were lit along the shore and fireworks arced high into the night sky.

There is a persistent legend that crews of passing ships claimed to have seen ghost like figures climbing the iron ladder on the side of the tower and sometimes hearing strange voices. Some sailors said the ghost were shouting at them to, "Keep away." Keepers complained of strange sounds as they went about their daily tasks, as if the men killed on the fallen tower were trying to communicate with them. There is also a tale about a keeper who became so despondent he slit his throat with a razor blade.

Baked Beans With Maple And Rum–Historic

4 cups dry navy beans

3 quarts water

1 teaspoon baking soda

1 pound salt pork or ham

1 large onion

1 teaspoon dry mustard

1 cup maple syrup

1 tablespoon salt

4 apples, cored and unpeeled

1 cup maple sugar

1/2 cup butter

1/2 cup dark rum

Rinse beans, cover with cold water, soak over night. Pour beans and water into large pot. Add baking soda and more water to cover beans. Bring to a boil uncovered and boil until some of the skins fall off when you blow on them. Line a bean pot with thin slices of ham or pork, pour in beans and water. Roll onion in dry mustard completely and bury it in middle of beans and water. Pour maple syrup and salt over top. Bake at 325 degrees for 4 to 5 hours. At the start of the last hour, place whole apples on top as close together as possible. Cream maple sugar and butter together and spread over the top of apples. Pour rum over top just before serving.

Recipe Courtesy: Massachusetts Maple Producers Association, www.massmaple.org

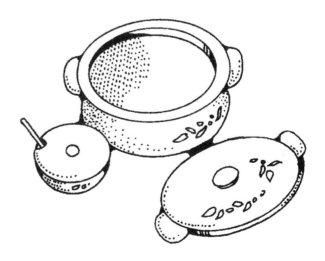

Monomoy Lighthouse
Monomoy Island, Massachusetts

Author's Collection

The waters offshore from the old Monomoy Point Lighthouse have long been a graveyard of ships. South of Monomoy Island is Pollack Rip, a place of strong tidal currents very dangerous to sailors. It is said it was the local currents and shoals that caused the Pilgrims to sail into Cape Cod Bay rather than continue on to Virginia as originally intended.

Monomoy Point is about eight miles from Chatham, near the south edge of Cape Cod. The first lighthouse on Monomoy Point, built in 1823, was the fifth light on Cape Cod. The design was common to others in the area, with a wooden tower and iron lantern room perched on the roof of a brick keeper's house. An inspector in 1842 recorded that Monomoy Point was, "one of the most important locations on the coast of the United States. Thousands of vessels pass here annually amid the numerous and very dangerous shoals that obstruct navigation." He also noted that the light was in bad condition and recommended a new one be built.

In 1849 the new station was constructed, including a cast iron brick lined tower and wooden keeper's house. Eight years later the light received a new fourth order Fresnel lens.

Monomoy was always an isolated station however the men and their families were able to enjoy the bounty of the sea. Fish, clams, lobster and waterfowl were plentiful. The population of the lonely island increased in 1872 when two U.S. Life-Saving Service Stations were built at Monomoy.

Monomoy Light was discontinued in 1923 and the property sold into private hands. When the Cape Cod Canal opened in 1914 the power of the Chatham Light was increased making Monomoy Light superfluous. During World War II the Navy used the island as a bombing range.

The Massachusetts Audubon Society restored the light in 1964 with additional work done by the Lighthouse Preservation Society in 1988. A major blizzard and storm in 1978 slammed into the peninsula with enough power to cut it into two islands, North and South Monomoy. Today both are managed by the U.S. Fish and Wildlife Service. It is also known as a birdwatcher's paradise with over 300 species found there. Rare gray seals have also been breeding on the island.

Monomoy Cranberry Pie–Contemporary

2 cups whole washed cranberries

1/2 cup sliced almonds

1-1/2 cups sugar

1-1/2 sticks butter

2 eggs

1 cup flour

1-1/2 teaspoons almond extract

Wild cranberry bogs can be found between the dunes on South Monomoy Island as well as at nearby Harwich. Doubtless the old keepers and their families made good use of cranberries in a variety of ways.

Preheat oven to 375 degrees. Butter a 9 or 10-inch glass pie plate. On the bottom, pour in 2 cups of whole washed fresh cranberries. Sprinkle 1/2 cup of sugar and 1/2 cup of sliced almonds over the layer of cranberries and put aside.

Mix 1 cup of sugar and 1-1/2 sticks of melted butter. Add 2 beaten eggs, 1 cup flour, 1-1/2 teaspoons almond extract and mix together with a wire whisk. Pour mixture over berries and nuts. Bake for 35 minutes at 375 degrees. When baking is near done, berries should rise to the top (this will not happen if you use frozen berries). The texture is cake like. Serve in a bowl with fresh whipped cream.

Recipe Courtesy: Peter and Adele Geraghty, Asa Jones House, Harwich Center, Cape Cod, Massachusetts, www.asajoneshouse.com

Nauset Lighthouse
Eastham, Massachusetts

National Archives

The convoluted history of Nauset Light is one of the strangest in New England. The story begins in 1836 when the residents of Eastham petitioned the government to build a light at Nauset Beach. Eastham was originally named Nauset when founded in 1644.

The government agreed with the petition but because it was necessary to provide a unique characteristic from the nearby lights at Truro and the twin towers at Chatham, it was decided to build a station with three identical towers! The infamous Winslow Lewis received the contract to build them and after a mere 38 days of work, the 15-foot high, brick towers were finished. They were 150 feet apart and a small keeper's house was located nearby. They were quickly dubbed the "Three Sisters of Nauset!"

The lights had many critics. One inspector said a single red light would have been adequate. Another called them a, "…costly way of accomplishing that objective." A third inspector claimed all three could be replaced with a single flashing light.

In 1856 the towers received sixth order Fresnel lenses and in 1873 were upgraded to fourth order lenses. Beach erosion in 1892 forced the construction of three new wood towers further inland. Continued erosion resulted in moving the center tower in 1911 and selling the other two for use as summer cottages.

Weather at the Cape is very hard on structures and by 1923 the remaining tower was in a very deteriorated condition. To replace it the Board removed the discontinued cast iron twin tower at Chatham and assembled it at Nauset.

Nauset Light was automated in 1955 and the fourth order lens replaced with an aero beacon in 1981. The old Fresnel is on exhibit at the Cape Cod National Seashore Eastham Visitor Center. Erosion continued to be the deadly enemy of Nauset Light. The Coast Guard proposed in 1993 to discontinue the light because of both the rapidly advancing ocean and declining need for the beacon. The proposal sparked a storm of protest, resulting in the formation of the Nauset Light Preservation Society. Eventually the light was moved to a safe location. In the intervening years the National Park Service purchased the old three sisters towers, relocated them closer to the original site and restored them. They are now open to the public.

Ragout Of Beef With Cranberries–Contemporary

1 tablespoon of margarine

1 tablespoon oil

2 pounds lean stew meat

2 medium onions, chopped

2 cloves garlic, minced

8 ounces fresh mushrooms, sliced

3/4 cup port or red wine

3/4 cup beef stock

2 tablespoons red wine vinegar

1 tablespoon tomato paste

1-1/2 cups fresh cranberries (preferably from Cape Cod)

1/3 cup firmly packed light brown sugar

2 tablespoons flour

This is a favorite winter dish, one well calculated to enable the consumer to face the rigors of Cape Cod's chilling winds. Cranberries are native to Cape Cod.

Melt the butter or margarine and oil in a Dutch oven and brown the meat well on all sides. Stir in the onions, garlic and salt and pepper to taste. Add the mushrooms, port or red wine, vinegar, beef stock and tomato paste. Bring to a boil. Reduce the heat, cover and simmer for about 2 hours. (If making ahead, stop here and refrigerate or freeze, continue with the last part before serving.) Coarsely chop the cranberries with the brown sugar and flour in a food processor. Add to the stew and cook, stirring often, for 10 minutes more until thickened. Serve over buttered egg noodles. Serves 6.

Recipe Courtesy: Patricia Stone, Lighthouse Inn, West Dennis, Massachusetts, 02670, www.lighthouseinn.com

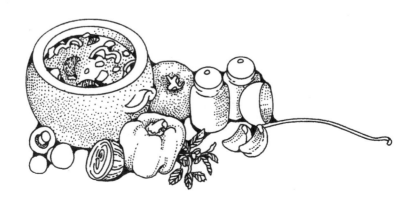

Nobska Lighthouse
Woods Hole, Massachusetts

U.S. Coast Guard Collection

Nobska Light, one of the most popular lighthouses on Cape Cod, is right on the border between Buzzard's Bay and Vineyard Sound. From its perch high on the rocks above Woods Hole, it is in clear view of the ferries running between Woods Hole and New Bedford for Martha's Vineyard. Today Woods Hole is best known as the home of the Woods Hole Oceanographic Institute of international fame.

The original lighthouse was built in 1828. It was a familiar Cape Cod structure with the light tower projecting through the center of the roof. This style of lighthouse proved to be a poor design due to difficulties in effectively supporting the tower with the internal framing of the house. Roof leaks at the tower roof juncture were common. The classic lighthouse design of a tower at one end of the house historically proved more efficient. Illumination was provided by a ten-lamp reflector chandelier.

Vessel traffic around Nobska Point was always high. On a single day in 1864, the keeper logged 188 passing vessels. Due to deterioration of the original structure, in 1876 the light was replaced with a new 40-foot iron tower and separate quarters. A fifth order Fresnel provided the illumination. In 1888 the small lens was replaced with a fourth order lens, which is still in place today.

The light was automated by the Coast Guard in 1985 and is presently the home of the Group Commander of the Woods Hole Coast Guard Base. During the summer the local Coast Guard Auxiliary takes charge of tours of the grounds and tower.

Ginger Bread Pancakes—Contemporary

1 cup flour

1-1/2 teaspoons baking powder

1/2 teaspoon cinnamon

Dash cloves

2/3 cup skim milk

2 tablespoons molasses

1 tablespoon vegetable oil

1 egg lightly beaten

Pancakes are a wonderful treat anytime, breakfast, lunch or dinner! Steaming hot from the griddle and covered with a favorite topping, they are a great way to fuel up for a hard day of work or play.

Combine ingredients and stir until smooth. Make small pancakes. Serve with homemade whipped cream. Yield: Many

Recipe Courtesy: Llona and Bill Geise, Inn at One Main, Falmouth, MA, 02540
www.innatonemain.com

Race Point Lighthouse
Provincetown, Massachusetts

U.S. Coast Guard Collection

Race Point Lighthouse, at the northern tip of Cape Cod, is one of the most famous Massachusetts lights. It marked a point notorious for treacherous currents. In a bye gone maritime age, such currents were often called "races" thus the name.

Local townspeople started lobbying for a light as early as 1808 but it wasn't until 1816 that it was finally built and operating. The 25-foot high rubble tower was only the third light built on the Cape.

Like all of the lights before the Fresnel age, the beacon was dim and often difficult to see. When a fourth order Fresnel lens was installed in 1855, the improvement was dramatic. By 1875 the old rubble tower had deteriorated markedly and it clearly needed rebuilding or replacing. The following year a 45-foot tall cast iron tower lined with brick was constructed.

At one time a small fishing community was at Race Point, but as the years passed, it gradually faded away. By the turn of the century, the keeper's children had to trudge two and a half long miles across the lonely sand dunes to get to school.

The light was electrified in 1957 and automated in 1978. In 1995 the light, keeper's house and surrounding property were leased to the American Lighthouse Foundation. After being refurbished by volunteers, the lighthouse is now open to overnight stays under rustic conditions.

Race Point Clam Chowder-Historic

3 ounces salt pork, rind discarded and the salt pork cut crosswise into 1/4 inch strips

1 small onion, chopped

2 small red potatoes

1 cup water

25 shucked medium hard-shelled clams chopped, reserving 3/4 cup liquid

1-1/2 cups half and half, scalded

Originally spurned by early colonists, clams were soon recognized as a tasty treat and became a sought after commodity.

Rinse and pat dry the salt pork. Sauté the salt pork in a heavy saucepan over moderately high heat, stirring until it is golden. Transfer it to towels to drain and save 1-1/2 tablespoons of the fat. Cook the onion in the remaining pan fat over moderately low heat, stirring until it is softened and stir in the potatoes cut into 1/2 inch cubes and the water. Simmer the mixture covered for ten minutes or until the potatoes are just tender, then boil it, uncovered for 12 minutes or until the liquid is evaporated. Stir in the clams and the reserved liquid and simmer the mixture for 2 minutes. Stir in the half and half and salt pork into the clam mixture and season the chowder with salt and pepper. Yield: 4 cups

Recipe Courtesy: The Old Lightkeeper

Scituate Lighthouse
Scituate, Massachusetts

Scituate Harbor has long been home to shipbuilders, lobstermen and fishermen. In response to the strong maritime activity, Scituate Lighthouse was built at Cedar Point and lit for the first time on December 17, 1811.

Scituate Lighthouse is famous for the daring actions of the lighthouse keeper's daughters during the War of 1812. As the story goes, one day their father Simeon Bates was gone from the light, leaving his daughters Abigail and Rebecca alone. The two girls saw the British warship *La Hogue* approach the harbor and anchor. Soon five boats filled with sailors were rowing toward the lighthouse. Knowing the men were coming to destroy the light and perhaps burn the town, the girls took quick action. Grabbing a fife and drum that had been left at the light by local militia, they hid behind some bushes and played Yankee Doodle. The closer the boats came to shore the louder the girls played. Apparently thinking they were rowing into an ambush by American soldiers, the boats fled back to the ship. Two brave young girls, known as the "American Army of Two", saved Scituate.

Shipwrecks in the area continued in part because mariners confused Boston Light and Scituate Light. The height of the tower was raised to 40 feet in 1827 in an effort to provide better visibility. Scituate Light was discontinued on November 15, 1860 when the new light at Minot's Ledge became operational. In 1917 the Town of Scituate purchased the old lighthouse from the government for preservation as an historic site. Custody and administration of the light was given to the Scituate Historical Society in 1968.

Irish Moss Pudding–Historic

1/2 cup Irish moss

1 pint milk

1 teaspoon vanilla extract

1/4 cup maple syrup

1 egg white, stiffly beaten

1 pint whipping cream, stiffly beaten

Scituate is famous for its "Irish mossing" history. Irish moss is one of 80 red algae growing in the world but the only one that after processing can be used as an emulsifier or thickening agent in foods, medicines and cosmetics. For example, without Irish moss, ice cream would separate into layers and chocolate powder would stick to the sides of a chocolate milk bottle.

A Boston fisherman discovered Irish moss in Scituate in the late 1840s. Knowing it's rare value, he organized a group of his friends to begin to harvest the black, slimy gold. Using 14-foot long rakes, the men pulled it from the rocks during the short period two hours before low tide to two hours after. By the 1880s Scituate was supplying all of the Irish moss used is the United States.

Cover the dried moss with cold water and soak for 15 minutes. Remove debris, drain and remove any additional foreign material. Tie the Irish moss in a square of cheesecloth. Put milk and vanilla in top of a double boiler; suspend the cheesecloth bag in the milk mixture to a boil. Reduce the heat and let simmer, at the same time stirring and regularly pressing the bag against the side of the container with a spoon. After 20 minutes, remove the mixture from the heat and discard the bag.

Let stand for about 5 minutes, add maple syrup and stir in beaten egg white. Ladle the mixture into dessert dishes, cover and refrigerate. Before serving, top with whipped cream, which may be sweetened with confectioners sugar and a few drops of vanilla. Yield: Serves four.

Recipe Courtesy: John Galluzo, Scituate Historical Society, Scituate, Massachusetts 02066

Thatcher Island Twin Lights
Rockport, Massachusetts

Author's Collection

Thatcher Island received it's name as the result of the 1635 wreck of the vessel *Watch And Wait* in a terrible storm near the island. The only survivors of the 23 people aboard were Anthony Thatcher and his wife Elizabeth. All four of their children were lost along with his cousin, his wife and their six children. In recompense for his loss, the General Court of Massachusetts awarded the lonely island to him. Thereafter, it was known as Thatcher's Woe, later evolving into Thatcher's Island.

The Province of Massachusetts purchased the island from the Thatcher family in 1771 for the purpose of erecting twin 45-foot tall light towers. They were the first lights not marking a harbor entrance in the colonies and the last built under British rule.

Congress authorized the rebuilding of the towers in 1859. The result was two 124-foot cut granite towers, each with a first order Fresnel lens. Considering the island's elevation, the lights were 164-feet above sea level.

In 1864, Alexander Bray, a disabled Civil War veteran, was appointed keeper as a reward for his battle service. The day before Christmas 1865, an assistant keeper was struck down by a dangerous fever. To save his life, Bray and his other assistant took him to the mainland for medical aid. Bray's wife Maria was left on the island with her young nephew and two small children. Keeper Bray anticipated a quick trip, perhaps taking a couple of hours.

Before long the weather turned dreadfully foul. A heavy snowstorm struck the island, blotting out the sight of the shore and reducing visibility to near zero. When the men didn't return Maria knew they had missed the island and were lost at sea. All she could do to help was fire up the lights.

Maria was desperately worried about her children too. One was a toddler and the other still confined to a crib. Wrapping the older child up in a blanket against the piercing cold, she picked him up into her arms. She forced her way through snowdrifts to the south tower 300 yards distant. After catching her breath, she climbed the 156 steps to the lantern. Carefully trimming the wick, she lit the lantern then wound the clockworks to set the lens rotating. She returned to the keeper's house, rested and repeated the task for the north tower. Every five hours, she repeated the trip, until 5:00 a.m. when she fell exhausted into a chair and slept. At 7:00 a.m. her husband woke her and reportedly her first words were to ask if the lights were still burning. He replied, "If they were not, I would not be here!"

The north tower was eliminated in 1932 as an economy measure. The remaining tower was automated in 1980 and the lens removed to the Coast Guard Academy Museum. Of seven twin lights on the Atlantic coast, Thatcher Island was the last still in use when the Coast Guard closed the north tower.

The Thatcher Island Association was founded in 1983 to help save the lights. In 1989 the north light was restored and opened to the public. As a private aid to navigation and pairing it with the Coast Guard operated south tower, Thatcher Island is the only operating twin tower system in the U.S.

Dottie's Famous Lighthouse Cookies—Historic

1 cup butter

1 cup granulated sugar

3 egg yolks

2-1/2 cups sifted flour

1 teaspoon vanilla

White icing

Red cinnamon candies

Every good kitchen needs a cookie jar and every cookie jar needs cookies. These are especially appropriate for filling a lighthouse kitchen cookie jar.

Cream butter and gradually beat in sugar. Beat in eggs, one at a time. Add flour and vanilla. Chill. Roll to 1/8 inch thickness. Cut with a lighthouse cookie cutter. Bake 10-12 minutes at 350 degrees. Cool. Decorate with icing and put a red candy in the lantern room area or yellow one, which ever is preferred. Yield: about 60 cookies.

Recipe Courtesy: Dottie Carroll, Rockport, Massachusetts

Block Island Southeast Lighthouse Block Island, Rhode Island

U.S. Coast Guard Collection

Block Island is a dozen miles off the Rhode Island coast and the same distance from the eastern tip of Long Island, New York. The island runs about seven miles long and three miles across at its widest point. The reefs and shoals around the island are notorious for shipwrecks. Between 1819-1838, 59 vessels were lost in the area.

In response to these maritime disasters, the Lighthouse Service built the North Light in 1829 and Southeast Light in 1875. The latter light was classed as a primary seacoast light and was the highest in New England.

The design of Southeast Light was very close to that of Cleveland Light on Lake Erie built in 1870. Southeast Light was a blend of Italian and Gothic Revival styles, a mixture that makes the facility nearly unique in the Lighthouse Service. The octagonal tower is attached to a two and a half story duplex residence. Both are made of brick with granite trim. The light was first exhibited on February 1, 1875. Because of the importance of the light, the largest lens available, a first order fixed Fresnel, was installed.

The hurricane of September 21, 1938, the worst ever to strike New England, caused great damage to the station. The radio beacon tower was knocked down, oil house destroyed and windows blown out. Since electric power was lost, the keepers had to hand crank the lens for two days.

Southeast Light was deactivated in 1990, replaced with a steel tower and lexan optic. By this time the steady erosion of the cliffs had moved to within 50 feet of the lighthouse. It was originally over 300 feet distant. An energetic and dedicated group of volunteers raised $2 million to move the lighthouse to a safe location 300 feet from the cliff.

In 1994, the beacon was restored to the lighthouse and three years later Southeast Light was named a National Historic Landmark. Today the Block Island Southeast Lighthouse Foundation operates a small museum and gift shop in the lighthouse and offers tours of the tower during the summer.

Block Island Baked Bluefish–Contemporary

3 3-pound bluefish, cleaned, leaving the heads and tails intact

1 teaspoon salt

1 teaspoon freshly ground pepper, or to taste

2 large carrots, sliced thin

1 large onion, chopped

5 ribs of celery, sliced thin

1/2 cup coarsely chopped fresh dill

1/2 cup coarsely chopped fresh basil leaves

1 cup coarsely chopped fresh parsley leaves

1/2 stick (1/2 cup) unsalted butter, melted

1-1/4 cups dry white wine

Bluefish are a migratory fish found along the U.S. coast from Maine to Florida. Voracious predators, they can reach a size in excess of 30 pounds. A tremendous sport fish, some are commercially harvested.

Sprinkle the bluefish inside and out with the salt and the pepper. In a large bowl combine the carrots, onion, celery, dill, basil and parsley. Spoon three fourths of the stuffing into the fish, reshape the fish, pressing them closed and arrange them cut sides down in a baking dish just large enough to hold them.

Arrange the remaining stuffing around the fish and pour the butter and the wine over the fish.

Bake the fish in the middle of a preheated 350-degree oven for 35 minutes or until they just flake. Transfer them carefully with spatulas to a platter and spoon the stuffing around them. Yield: 8-10 servings.

Recipe Courtesy: The 1661 Inn and Hotel Manisses Bed and Breakfast and Restaurant, Block Island, www.blockisland.com/biresorts/

Lime Rock Lighthouse
Newport, Rhode Island

U.S. Coast Guard Collection

Lime Rock Lighthouse is well known for the exploits of Ida Lewis, considered the most heroic of all American female lightkeepers. Ida was born in 1842 in Newport. Her father was Horsa Lewis, a Revenue Marine pilot who became the first Lime Rock lightkeeper in 1854. Lime Rock was strictly a harbor light using a diminutive sixth order Fresnel lens. A small tower was attached to the dwelling.

When a two-story keeper's house was built on the island in 1858, Horsa quickly moved his family to the island. Four months later, he suffered what is thought to have been a debilitating stroke. Since he was no longer able to tend the light, his wife assumed the job.

When Ida moved to Lime Rock she knew very little about lightkeeping or boat handling. But as the second oldest of four children, she soon learned how to tend the light and gained boat-handling skills by rowing the younger children to school and back as well as fetching supplies.

Ida showed a remarkable ability to make rescues. In 1859, when only 16 years old, she used the rowing boat to save four young men from a capsized sailboat. Seven years later she saved three sailors from a sinking skiff.

When her father died in 1872 her mother was appointed in his place and in 1879 Ida was appointed keeper. Her rescues continued. By the time she died at the light in 1911, at age 69 it was claimed she had saved 35 people. During her career she received numerous recognition, including the Gold Life-Saving medal in 1880. On July 4, 1869, Newport held a parade in her honor and presented her with many gifts, including a custom made rowing boat. Her many awards never "went to her head." She kept many of them in a small workbasket in her kitchen and referred to them only as her "baubles."

The Rhode Island legislature officially changed the name of Lime Rock to Lewis Rock in 1924 to honor the remarkable keeper. Later the Lighthouse Service renamed the light the Ida Lewis Light. This was the only time the name of a lighthouse was changed to honor a keeper.

On November 1, 1996 the Coast Guard accepted delivery of the *Ida Lewis*, WLM 551, the lead ship of the new Keeper Class buoy tenders built by Marinette Marine Corporation in Marinette, Wisconsin.

Scallops Newport–Contemporary

4 ounces sea scallops

4 ounces mushrooms

2 ounces fresh spinach

2 ounces smoked salmon

2 fluid ounces beurre blanc

Beurre Blanc (white butter sauce)

1/8 cup shallots, minced

1/2 cup white wine

1 cup heavy whipping cream

1/2 tablespoon salt

1/8 cup blond roux

1/4 pound unsalted butter, cut in small cubes

1/8 cup lemon juice

1/4 tablespoon white pepper

Sauté scallops. When ready add mushrooms, spinach and smoked salmon and toss. Add Beurre Blanc and toss well. Serve.

Beurre Blanc sauce:
Cook shallots in wine in large pot until wine is reduced by 1/4. Add cream and salt and bring it to a boil, then reduce heat. Watch it very closely because it will boil over quickly. Add the blond roux and whisk well.

Whisk in butter piece by piece until all is incorporated. Add lemon juice, salt and pepper. Keep warm in a bain marie.

Note: When bringing cream to a boil, it must be watched, as it will boil over very quickly.

Recipe Courtesy: Little Old Lightkeeper

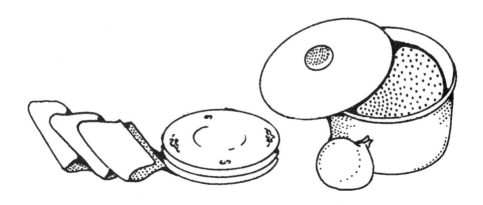

Rose Island Lighthouse Newport, Rhode Island

U.S. Coast Guard Collection

Rose Island Lighthouse is a very special lighthouse. It is not remembered for its history, although it has a colorful one. Nor for it's importance as a major beacon. Since it is only a minor harbor light. But nonetheless, it is still special.

Rose Island is in the middle of Narragansett Bay, barely a mile from Newport. The island is only 17 acres and most of the land is now a bird sanctuary, which completely surrounds the lighthouse. Although deactivated by the Coast Guard in 1971 when the large Newport suspension bridge was finished, it is now a popular destination for visitors wanting to experience primitive lighthouse living.

Operated by the Rose Island Lighthouse Foundation, the French Second Empire Revival style lighthouse was restored to its former glory, as a, "hands on museum" of the grand old days of lightkeeping. Overnight guests actually live in the museum and are required to clean up after themselves, changing bed linen and having their rooms back in order before the museum opens at 10:00 a.m.

The light looks like it did in 1912. There is no running water. Instead rainwater is collected by a cistern and then hand pumped to the kitchen for washing. Wind turbines provide all electricity, which limits it to low wattage interior lights only. The Rose Island Lighthouse Foundation prides itself on making the lighthouse as environmentally friendly as possible.

It was first illuminated on January 20, 1870 to guide vessels into and from Newport Harbor.

The island, less lighthouse, was sold in 1969 to a group of businessmen who planned to build a marina and condominium project. After the 1971 inactivation of the light, the property was leased to the University of Rhode Island as a marine research facility. Constant vandalism limited its usefulness and in the early 1980s it was taken over by the Rose Island Lighthouse Foundation. In 1993 the light in the old octagonal tower was again illuminated providing it's welcoming beacon far into the night.

Rose Island Clam Boil–Historic

white wine

mussels

clams

sweet potatoes

white potatoes

carrots

sausages and/or hot dogs

celery

onion

bass

lobster

This is more than just a recipe than a way to not only cook and prepare a great meal but also how to get it! It also illustrates how Rose Island guests can fully experience the "turn of the century" environment.

Start with a squid jig. Catch a squid then put it on a big hook to catch a striped bass. Scale, gut and fillet the bass. You can put some of it on the grill and brush it with lemon butter until cooked. Serve hot. Easy enough? That is just the beginning.

Put the fish's head, bones and organs into bait bag inside a lobster trap and lower it from the dock. The next day pull the trap out and throw any female lobsters back but keep the males.

Pour a cup of white wine into a big pot, and then add lots of clean mussels and some clams (as they cook they'll open up and make more "liquor" to steam the rest of the things in the pot). Add sweet potatoes, white potatoes and carrots (cut into big pieces but still in their skins), different kinds of sausages and/or hot dogs (what ever you like or have on hand), plus celery, onions, some of that good ol' bass wrapped up in brown paper so it doesn't fall apart and the lobsters of course. Then put the extra white potato on top. Quantities depend entirely on what's on hand and how many people you're trying to feed. Figure at least one big handful of shellfish and one piece of each item for each person.

Put the lid on tight and steam for about 35-40 minutes or until the top potato is done. You can also put corn in the pot, but we get such good sweet corn here that it is too good to cook it that long, so we steam it separately for just a few minutes.

Serve everything with melted butter and don't forget that broth from the pot!

Recipe Courtesy: Charlotte Johnson, Rose Island Lighthouse Foundation, P.O. Box 1419, Newport, Rhode Island, 02840-0997, www.RoseIslandLighthouse.org

Execution Rocks Lighthouse
Long Island Sound, New York

U.S. Coast Guard Collection

The very name Execution Rocks evokes fear and dread! There is also confusion as to how it gained such an unsavory reputation. One theory maintains so many vessels were "executed" on the reef, old British naval charts noted it as "Executioners Rock." Another legend claims the name came from the British practice of executing American prisoners during the Revolution by chaining them to the rocks at low tide and waiting for the rising water to drown the condemned men.

Congress appropriated $25,000 for a 55-foot high granite light tower on the reef in 1847. Prior to then, there were unofficial beacons on the rock but they were unreliable and weak. By 1850 the new tower was finished and illuminated. A fourth order Fresnel was added in 1856 and keeper's quarters built in 1868.

A fire of unknown origin in 1918 caused significant damage, destroying the engine house and machinery, burning the roof off the oil house and damaging the keeper's house. There were other incidents. The steamer *Maine* smashed into the rocks in December 1920 during a snowstorm, narrowly missing the lighthouse. All 14 people aboard the steamer reached safety at the light. Execution Rocks Light was automated on December 5, 1979.

Local fishermen have alleged the ghostly spirits of both patriots and shipwreck victims still haunt the rocks, especially on dark and stormy nights. It was also argued that because of the light's sordid past, a keeper could be relieved from duty at the lighthouse just by asking.

Death By Chocolate~Contemporary

4 eggs

1 cup sour cream

1/2 cup water

1/2 cup oil

1 package chocolate cake mix

1 package chocolate instant pudding

12 ounces semisweet chocolate chips

Confectioners sugar

Beat eggs, sour cream, water and oil together in a large bowl until thoroughly mixed. Add cake mix and pudding mix. Beat until smooth. Stir in chocolate chips. Pour into bundt or tube pan and bake at 350 degrees for 1 hour. When cool, sift powdered sugar on top of cake or frost with chocolate glaze and sprinkle with chopped nuts. Variation: replace 1/4 cup water with Grand Mariner. Serves 8-10.

Recipe Courtesy: Pastry Wiz, www.pastrywiz.com/ archive/deathby.htm

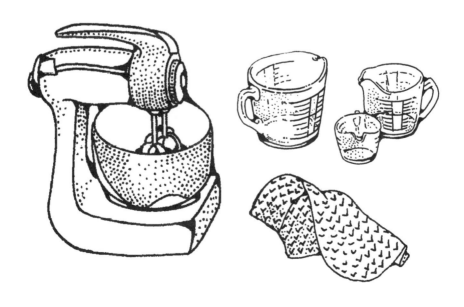

Fire Island Lighthouse
Fire Island, New York

U.S. Coast Guard Collection

Fire Island Light was once one of the most important lights in America. Soaring 168-feet high, for many European immigrants bound for New York City it was the first sight of the New World and their new opportunities.

Congress appropriated $40,000 for the light in 1857 and on November 1, 1858 it was lit for the first time. As with all major seacoast lights, a first order Fresnel lens occupied the lantern room. Because of it's location, in 1868 Western Union established a telegraph office at the light. The office would report vessels passing the light to shipping offices at New York City.

The original light at Fire Island was a 74-foot octagonal tower equipped with lamps and reflectors. Constructed of Connecticut River blue split stone, it was finished in 1826. It was torn down when the new tower was built and the stone used in a terracing project around the tower base. The littoral drift of Fire Island is spectacular. When the 1858 tower was built, it was next to the inlet. Now it is six miles to the west.

The light was electrified in 1939 and first order Fresnel replaced by an aero beacon. Fire Island Light was decommissioned on December 31, 1973. A replacement aid was placed on top of a local water tower.

Abandoned without maintenance, the old tower deteriorated and in 1981 it was declared beyond repair and demolition was considered. Lighthouse preservationists reacted strongly to the government's neglect and in 1982 the Fire Island Lighthouse Preservation Society formed which eventually raised $1.2 million for restoration. National Park Service acquired site management from the Coast Guard in 1983 and in 1985-86 the keeper's house became a museum. Full circle came on May 26, 1986 when the light was returned to the old tower where it belongs.

Long Island Steamed Mussels–Contemporary

2 quarts mussels (approximately 48 mussels)

3 tablespoons olive oil

1 onion, small, sliced thin

4 cloves garlic, pressed

4 stalks celery, including tops, chopped

8 ounces wine, dry white

1/2 teaspoon parsley, chopped fine

Seafood lovers often forget the lonely mussel, yet they can be incredibly tasty! Try this recipe to see just how good they can be!

Rinse mussels and remove the beards. Heat olive oil in a heavy pot. Add onion, pressed garlic and chopped celery to the oil. Sauté until onion becomes translucent. Add mussels and wine and cover pot tightly. Allow mussels to steam over high heat for approximately 5 minutes, shaking pot occasionally. Turn heat off and allow to stand for 2-3 minutes. Remove cover and discard any mussels which have not opened. Sprinkle with parsley and serve with broth for dipping.

Recipe Courtesy: New York Seafood Council, 252 East Montauk Highway, Hampton Bays, NY 11946

Montauk Point Lighthouse
Montauk Point, New York

Avery Collection

Montauk Point Lighthouse is one of the most famous American lights. Located on the extreme eastern tip of Long Island, it takes its name from the local Montauk Indians. The area is well suited for a lighthouse. During the Revolutionary War, the British occupied eastern Long Island and always kept a bonfire burning on the bluff as a beacon for their patrolling warships.

As trade increased following the Revolution, Montauk Point was increasingly recognized as one of the most dangerous places along the coast. In 1792, Congress purchased land on which to erect a lighthouse and in 1795 President Washington approved the funding for construction. The following November 5, the new light was finished. Its builder was John McComb Jr. of New York City, who had earlier constructed the lighthouse at Cape Henry, Virginia. Montauk Point Lighthouse is the oldest light in the state and the fourth oldest in the United States. Constructed of sandstone blocks from Connecticut, the walls at the base of the original 80-foot tower are six feet thick narrowing to three feet at the top. A two-story keeper's house was also erected.

Until construction of the Statue of Liberty in New York Harbor in 1886, Montauk Point Light stood as the symbol of the New World to immigrants from Europe. It was the first man-made structure they saw as they approached New York.

The tower was rebuilt in 1860 and increased to its present 110-foot height. Like all early lights, the original illumination was the lamp-reflector system. In 1857, a first order Fresnel lens was installed which in turn was replaced with a 3-1/2 order bivalve Fresnel in 1903. This lens has since been replaced with a DCH-224 aero-beacon.

The lighthouse has been witness to many shipwrecks. One was inadvertently caused by the Lighthouse Service. In January 1858 the new Ponquogue Light was established to the west of Montauk and the characteristics of Montauk changed from fixed to flashing. Ponquogue Light was given the fixed characteristic. A month later, the full rigged ship *John Milton* arrived off Ponquogue Light in a heavy gale. Unaware of either the new light or changed characteristics, they mistook Ponquogue's fixed beam for Montauk Point and smashed into the beach, killing all aboard.

Today the light is maintained by the Montauk Historical Society as a museum.

Montauk Scallops–Contemporary Version of Historic Recipe

2 pounds sea scallops

2 tablespoons butter and 2 tablespoons olive oil (or 4 tablespoons olive oil)

1 scant cup fresh bread crumbs

Salt, pepper, Old Bay seasoning to taste

Fresh dill, chopped

White wine and a little lemon juice or just white wine

Sea scallops are bivalve shellfish found in deep water from the Gulf of the St. Lawrence to coastal North Carolina. Left undisturbed, the sea scallop will lie quietly on the ocean floor. If disturbed, they will "clap" their shells together and "scoot" out of harms way. The large white muscle in the center of the scallop is the meat and is extremely tasty.

Mix the seasonings with the bread crumbs and roll the scallops in the mixture.

Add butter and oil (or oil alone) to hot frying pan and heat to very hot but not smoking.

Sauté the scallops for 5 minutes or less and transfer to a warm serving dish.

Add wine (and lemon juice if using it) to pan and cook until slightly reduced and creamy.

Pour sauce over scallops, add dill, stir and serve hot. Yield: 4 servings.

Recipe by: Annemarie Leber, courtesy Montauk Lighthouse Society, http://www.montauklighthouse.com

Race Rock Lighthouse
Long Island Sound, New York

Author's Collection

Race Rock Lighthouse is a picturesque example of a gothic revival style light common to Northeast waters. Construction of the light took nearly eight years and an expenditure of nearly $277,000.

Race Rock marks part of the "Race," a deep and dangerous passage through an area of rocks and shallows. During a tide change water runs fast and powerfully through the passage, making it especially hazardous for shipping.

The first wreck on Race Rock happened in 1671 when the British warship *John And Lucy* struck it with the loss of several lives. In 1845 the steamer *Atlantic* plowed into it causing 45 deaths. Many other vessels met their end on the sharp rock of the "Race." Attempts to use buoys and an iron daymark to guide mariners failed. The swift currents swept them away.

Clearly a lighthouse was needed. Work on a rock foundation started in 1870. Even while under construction the Race proved dangerous. During blasting to level the foundation, an accidental explosion destroyed a contractors boat, killing several workers. Four years later construction of the actual lighthouse started. Progress was slow. Halting the work during the foul winter months, repairing storm damage and fighting gales, and waiting for materials, all caused delay.

Finally the lighthouse was finished in 1878 and it's fourth order Fresnel lens illuminated on January 1, 1879. The light was automated in 1978 and the Fresnel was replaced with an aero beacon.

Race Rock Cold Lobster Salad–Contemporary

Fresh lobster meat, chopped into bite sized pieces, (the amount depends upon how many people you are serving). Three generous portions per pound of fresh picked lobster meat.

1/2 cup celery, chopped per pound of lobster meat

Lemon juice to taste

Mayonnaise to taste

Salt and pepper to taste

This recipe is unique in that it is provided by the great, great granddaughter of Captain T. A. Scott, the builder of Race Rock Lighthouse. Whether Captain Scott ever had lobster salad prepared exactly in this manner is of course unknown, but he certainly had lobster!

The salad is delicious served on a toasted roll accompanied by fresh cole slaw or served atop a fresh green garden salad.

Chop lobster into bite sized pieces. Mix with celery, then add lemon juice, mayonnaise, salt and pepper. Serve on a variety of toasted buns, breads or green salad.

Recipe Courtesy: Susan Eshenfelder, Captain Scott's Lobster Dock, 80 Hamilton St., New London, CT 06320

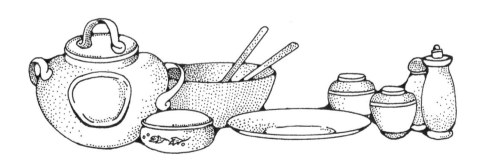

Robbins Reef Lighthouse
New York Harbor, New York

U.S. Coast Guard Collection

The first light at Robbins Reef was built in 1839 to help guide ships past a dangerous rock ridge and through the Ambrose Channel. Staten Island is about two and a half miles distant to the north. It is the most isolated of all the lights on the New York approaches. The old stone tower was replaced with a four tiered conical iron light in 1883. The new light was 56 feet tall and used a fourth order Fresnel lens with a range of a dozen miles.

Quarters were reasonably comfortable for an offshore light. A galley and mess room were on the main floor and two bedrooms above. Tiny windows were cut into the circular walls to allow for natural light. Davits on the side held the keeper's boat and a 30-foot vertical iron ladder provided access to the light.

The most famous keeper was Kate Walker, known as the grand old lady of the east coast. In 1883 her husband Jacob was appointed keeper and she became his official assistant. When he died in 1886 and she was appointed in his place, her eldest son assumed the assistant's job. Reputedly her husband's last words to her as he lay dying were, "Mind the light Kate." And so she did, for the next 33 years, retiring in 1919 at age 73. There was resistance to her appointment. She was only four foot ten inches tall and 100 pounds, a mere slip of a woman. Surely she couldn't do the job! How wrong the critics were.

Kate was a German immigrant who met her husband when he was the assistant keeper at Sandy Hook Lighthouse. She was a waitress at the boarding house where he took his meals. After a time, he wooed and won her and they lived a comfortable life at Sandy Hook lighthouse. When he transferred to Robbins Reef she reluctantly accompanied him, but hated the new light. For a time she refused to even unpack her trunks.

During her tenure she was credited with saving fifty lives of people on distress in the bay, as well as maintaining an exemplary light. It was said she could identify every steamer by the sound of its fog whistle. She also raised two children at the light and rowed them two miles to school and back every day.

Robbins Reef Light was automated in 1966 and is still an active aid to navigation. In 1997 the Coast Guard accepted delivery of the *Katherine Walker*, WLM 552, a 175-foot Keeper Class buoy tender built by Marinette Marine Corporation in Marinette, Wisconsin. Kate's fame lives on.

Kate Walker Stew—Contemporary

10 pounds Beef Chuck, diced, thawed

3 tablespoons salt

2 teaspoons black pepper

1/3 teaspoon dehydrated garlic

1 teaspoon ground cinnamon

1 teaspoon ground allspice

2 tablespoons brown sugar, packed

2 gallons hot water

2-1/2 pounds frozen green peas

2 large onions

Tomatoes, canned and cut into pieces

1 cup cornstarch

1-1/2 pint cold water

To warm a buoy deck crew while servicing seasonal Aids to Navigation on the Hudson River on a cold, windy, December day.

1. Place meat in 2 pans

2. Combine salt, pepper, garlic, cinnamon, allspice and brown sugar; sprinkle an equal quantity over meat in each pan.

3. Cook in a 400º F oven for about 1 hour.

4. Add 1gallon water to each pan. Cover, simmer 1-1/2 hours in 350º F oven.

5. Add peas, onion and tomatoes to meat in pan. Stir to combine. Cover, simmer until peas and beef are tender.

6. Blend cornstarch and water to make a smooth paste. Slowly add mixture to ingredients in pan. Blend thoroughly. Cook 5 minutes or until thickened.

Recipe Courtesy: U.S. Coast Guard Cutter *Kate Walker*

Shinnecock Lighthouse
Shinnecock Bay, New York

U.S. Coast Guard Collection

Although commonly called Shinnecock Light, this station was also known as Ponquogue (also Pon Quogue) Point Light and Great West Bay Light. During its heyday, it was an important aid for vessels entering and leaving Long Island's Shinnecock Bay.

Congress authorized the light in 1854 but construction of the 160-foot brick tower was delayed until a proper site could be secured. The completed light was first illuminated on June 1, 1858.

Shinnecock Light actually caused a shipwreck when a ship not realizing it even existed, confused the tower with Montauk Point Light and navigated accordingly.

The light's usefulness was relatively short lived. Shifting channels and sandbars so altered the geology of the area that on August 1, 1931 the light was extinguished for the last time. The Coast Guard wanted to expand their station and the old tower was not part of the plans for the new facility, so it would have to go. The Coast Guard alleged the tower was "unsafe." Local residents protested the charge vigorously, stating it was as strong as the day it was built as well as being an important local historical landmark. A local congressman won a short reprieve from the Coast Guard but on December 23, 1948 it was demolished. So ended an era.

Long Island Fisherman Stew–Historic

2 pounds cod fillets (monkfish, sea bass, blackfish or porgy)

1 tablespoon margarine or butter

1 cup onion, chopped

1 clove garlic, crushed

2 cans tomatoes, undrained, cut up (each can should be 1 pound or 16 ounces)

3 cups water

1 teaspoon basil

1 teaspoon thyme

1/4 teaspoon red pepper, crushed

1 teaspoon salt

4 cups pumpkin or winter squash, cut into 1-inch cubes

2 ears corn, cut crosswise into 1-inch pieces

There is an old joke about a wife questioning why her husband never seemed to catch anything when he went fishing. His reply went along the lines of, "That's why it's called fishing and not catching!" This recipe gives the fisherman wide latitude in what he provides the cook. Basically, if its edible fish, it will work in this stew!

Cut fish fillets into 1 to 2 inch pieces. In a large saucepan melt margarine. Add onion and garlic and cook until tender. Add tomatoes, water, basil, thyme, red pepper, salt, pumpkin and corn. Cover and bring to a boil. Simmer 10-15 minutes or until pumpkin and corn are done. Add fish and continue to cook for 5-10 minutes or until fish turns opaque and begins to flake when tested with a fork.

Recipe Courtesy: New York Seafood Council, 252 East Montauk Highway, Hampton Bays, NY 11946

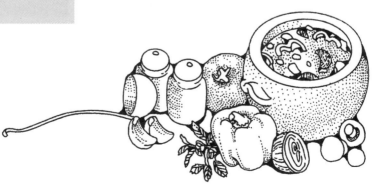

Absecon Inlet Lighthouse
Atlantic City, New Jersey

Avery Collection

When approaching from the ocean, much of the New Jersey coastline is low and hard to distinguish. Like that of North Carolina, long areas of offshore sandbars are common. Absecon Island was such an area. Shipwrecks were frequent and the local wreckers gained an unsavory reputation. Some people accused them of not only causing wrecks by showing a false light, but also robbing bodies of the victims. When the packet ship *Powhatten* wrecked at Absecon Beach in 1854 during a vicious northeast gale an estimated 300 people perished. Clearly a lighthouse would improve maritime safety along this deadly stretch of coast.

Following the *Powhatten* disaster Congress appropriated funding for the lighthouse. Construction on the tower started under the direction of Major Hartman Bache and later continued under Lieutenant George G. Meade. As a major general he would command Union forces at Gettysburg in 1863. Both Bache and Meade were U.S. Army Corp of Engineers officers. After the formation of the Lighthouse Board in 1852, Corp of Engineer officers were critical to the design and construction of "America's Castles." During this period of American history, the U.S. Military Academy at West Point, New York was nearly the only college producing competent engineers. By tradition, only the best and the brightest of the Army's officers received coveted commissions in the Corp of Engineers.

The brick light tower at Absecon stands 169 feet tall and was topped off with a first order Fresnel lens classifying it as a primary seacoast light. It was first lit on January 15, 1857. The value of the new light was quickly apparent. During the ten months following illumination there was not a single shipwreck in the area. Previously they were commonplace.

The Lighthouse Board directed the tower be painted white in 1872 to increase its visibility. In 1898 the daymark characteristic was changed to orange and black. The nearby town grew into the famous Atlantic City, the "Queen of the Shore Resorts." As the city expanded, it slowly grew around the lighthouse to the point that today the tower is in the middle of town!

Absecon Light was discontinued in 1933 and replaced with a beacon on the city's Steel Pier. The city took over the old light in 1948 and it has since been restored.

Salt Water Taffy–Contemporary

2 cups sugar

1 cup light corn syrup

1-1/2 cups water

1-1/2 teaspoons salt

2 teaspoons glycerin

2 tablespoons butter

2 teaspoons vanilla extract

Combine sugar, syrup, water, salt and glycerin in a buttered 3-quart heavy saucepan. Place on medium-high heat and stir until the sugar dissolves. Then cook without stirring to the hardball stage (260 degrees F). Remove from heat and add butter and flavoring.

Pour into a buttered, shallow pan. When cool enough to handle, pull taffy, wrap in waxed paper and store.

Recipe Courtesy: Patricia Zastera

Cape May Lighthouse
Cape May, New Jersey

The origins of the original Cape May Light are murky. There is some evidence a lighthouse could have been erected as early as 1744. What is known is that in 1821 Congress appropriated construction funding for a lighthouse in the area. Using brick carried down from Philadelphia, a 70-foot brick tower was finished in 1823. A fifteen lamp and reflector system provided the illumination. The lighthouse was discontinued in 1847 due to deterioration of the structure and beach erosion.

A new 94-foot tower was built in 1847 on a site 400 yards to the northeast. It too had a fifteen-lamp system. An 1851 inspection stated the tower was, "...rough and crudely built" and poorly maintained. The keeper was also untrained and had low morale. Poor construction caused the light to be abandoned in 1859 and the third and present tower constructed 1,000 feet further inshore. This 170-foot tower has walls eight feet thick at the base, tapering to two feet at the top. It was first illuminated on October 31, 1859.

Cape May Light was considered very important and one of nine lights the new (1852) Lighthouse Board decided should be upgraded to primary seacoast lights and equipped with first order Fresnel lenses. The other lights were at Capes Henlopen, Charles, Henry, Hatteras, Lookout, Fear, Romain and Charleston, South Carolina.

A first order Fresnel lens was installed in the new tower. Originally illuminated with kerosene lamps, in 1910 it was changed to incandescent oil vapor and electrified in 1938.

In 1945 the first order Fresnel was replaced by a 36-inch aero-beacon. The original Fresnel is on display at the Cape May County History Museum. The Mid-Atlantic Center for the Arts currently leases the lighthouse from the state and is actively restoring it.

Cape May is an old New Jersey seaside community nationally known for its Victorian architecture. During the height of the seaside resort era, Cape May was considered more "upscale" than Atlantic City. Visiting historic Cape May today is like stepping back in time to another age.

Cape May No Bake Chocolate Topped Nut Chews–Contemporary

6 cups (about 90) vanilla wafers, finely crushed

1 cup ground toasted almonds

1 cup butter, melted and cooked

1/2 cup sweetened condensed milk

1/4 teaspoon salt

2 cups chocolate chips

Vacationing in a Victorian resort city like Cape May can be a wonderful experience, made all the better by such a mouth-watering treat as these chocolate topped nut chews.

Combine crumbs, nuts, butter, condensed milk and salt. Mix well. Press into a greased rimmed 10 x 15 inch cooking pan. Melt chocolate chips and stir until smooth. Spread chips over crumb layer. Chill until firm. Cut into 2 x 1 inch bars. Yield: 72 bars.

Recipe Courtesy: Dane and Joan Wells, Queen Victoria Bed and Breakfast, 102 Ocean St., Cape May, NJ, 08204, www.queenshotel.com

Navesink Twin Lights
Atlantic Highlands, New Jersey

U.S. Coast Guard Collection

One of the most unique lighthouses in the U.S. is the Navesink Twin Lights in Atlantic Highlands, New Jersey. From a distance, the structure resembles a fortress. All that is missing are cannon on the battlements.

The original brownstone towers were built in 1828 with the intention that two lights approximately 100 yards apart would be distinct in appearance from the light at Sandy Hook and would assist shipping approaching New York harbor.

Both towers originally used lamps and reflectors. In 1841, the north tower was fitted with a first order Fresnel fixed lens and south tower with a second order revolving Fresnel lens. These were the first Fresnels ever used in an American lighthouse and their installation was directed by Congress as a test of the new system. The test was successful and when the towers were rebuilt in 1861 to a height of 73 feet, each tower received a first order fixed Fresnel lens. Sitting on a bluff nearly two hundred feet above the ocean the lights had a range of 22 nautical miles.

In 1898, the south lens was changed to a first order bivalve (clamshell) flashing Fresnel. Today the massive lens is on display in the old generator building. A primary navigation aid for New York, the Twin Lights became a testing station for many new technologies. In 1883, it was the first first order station to convert to kerosene as a fuel, increasing the available candlepower over the old lard oil. In 1898, the south tower was also the first light converted to electricity.

The Coast Guard decommissioned Navesink Twin Lights in 1952. A sixth order Fresnel was installed in the north tower in 1962 and it was reactivated as a private aid to navigation to honor the long history of the station. The facility became a New Jersey State Historic Site in 1960 and is presently a museum.

Bahr's Famous Lobster Bisque–Contemporary

1/4 cup butter

1/2 cup carrots, diced

1/2 cup celery, diced

1/3 cup onions, chopped finely

2 lobsters, 1-1/4 pounds each, separated into tail, claws and chest pieces

1/4 cup cognac

2 cups wine, white

2 cups water

2 garlic cloves, crushed

2 tablespoons tarragon, fresh, roughly chopped

1 bay leaf

28 ounces tomatoes, drained

Salt to taste

Pepper to taste

1/3 cup rice, long grain white

1/2 cup butter

1 tablespoon cognac or cooking sherry

1 cup cream, light

1 cup milk

Historic Bahr's Restaurant is in the shadow of the Navesink Twin Lights and the Sandy Hook Light. Doubtless many of the keepers and their families enjoyed this wonderful restaurant.

Melt butter in a large saucepan. Add the carrots, celery and onions and cook until soft, about 10 minutes. Add sections from lobsters to pan and saute until shells turn red. Remove pieces from pan when cool enough and remove meat from tails and claws and reserve it.

Chop shells into smaller pieces and add to pan. Add 1/4 cup cognac and ignite. Then add the white wine, water, garlic, tarragon and bay leaf. Crush the drained tomatoes with hands and add to the pot. Season with salt and pepper.

Simmer over low heat for 45 minutes, but do not allow liquid to boil. Remove as many pieces of shell as possible. Put soup through food mill and return milled broth to pan. Add the reserved lobster meat and rice. Simmer over low heat another 45 minutes or until reduced to 2 cups.

Pulse shells in a food processor until finely chopped. Melt butter in a sauté pan, add chopped shells and sauté 5 minutes. Strain, reserving butter and discarding shells.

Transfer reduced lobster-rice mixture to blender and puree. Strain the puree through a sieve over a mixing bowl and return broth to pot. Add the lobster butter and stir well.

Add cognac and heat for 5-7 minutes. Add the light cream and milk. Heat through, but do not boil. Yield: 8 servings.

Recipe Courtesy: Bahr's Restaurant, 2 Bay Ave., Highlands, NJ 07732, www.bahrs.com

Sandy Hook Lighthouse
Sandy Hook, New Jersey

National Archives

The need for the Light at Sandy Hook was identified very early. In 1679-80 the colonial governor of New York suggested to the governor of New Jersey that a light at the Hook was clearly needed. The suggestion was not acted on until 1761 when New York City merchants, distraught over the large number of ships lost in the area, decided to take action themselves. Obtaining the approval of the provincial council, they raised the construction money through a series of lotteries. The resulting structure is a rubble octagonal tower 29 feet in diameter at the base tapering to 15 feet at the top. Overall height is 103 feet. Illumination came from 48 oil lamps. Originally sited about 500 feet from the tip of the Hook, as the result of the slow build up of sand along the beach, the light is now about a mile and a half from the point. Each vessel entering or leaving the harbor was charged a light duty of three pence per ton to pay the operating costs of the light.

During the Revolution the light was a valuable asset for both sides. When the British fleet unexpectedly appeared off New York, the Rebels quickly removed the lamps to prevent their use by the enemy. The British responded by using improvised lamps. The Americans in turn tried to damage the tower with gunfire from ships but were driven away by the British.

Following the war, the light was placed back in full use and original lamps and reflectors restored. However it became a point of contention between New York and New Jersey. The problem was that the light was owned by New York interests but was on New Jersey soil. How could this be? The issue became moot when the federal government assumed responsibility for all lights in 1789.

In 1818 the ancient oil lamps were replaced with new lamps and reflectors, which were eventually replaced with a third order Fresnel in 1856. Repairs to the tower in 1857 included a new brick lining and iron steps replacing the old wood ones.

There is a strange legend concerning the lighthouse. Supposedly during construction work in 1857, an old cellar was opened and a skeleton sitting on a chair in front of a makeshift fireplace was discovered. Is the legend true or just imagination?

In 1889 Sandy Hook Light was the first light in America illuminated with electricity.

Sandy Hook was designated a National Historic Landmark in 1964. Today the light and surrounding Fort Hancock are part of the Gateway National Recreation Area. The light is still active and a third order Fresnel continues to occupy the lantern room. It is the oldest continuously operating lighthouse in America.

Breaded Flounder–Contemporary

1/2 pound fresh flounder

3 tablespoons Italian breadcrumbs

2 tablespoons Hellman's mayonnaise

1 tablespoon freshly minced parsley

A member of the flatfish family, flounder ranges from Nova Scotia to Florida. Although there are many ways to prepare them, this simple recipe is a favorite.

Preheat oven to 350 degrees. Place flounder on a greased baking dish or cookie sheet. Spoon some mayonnaise on top and spread out in a thin layer. Sprinkle lightly with breadcrumbs, parsley and salt and pepper. Turn flounder over and repeat on reverse side. Place in oven and bake for 6 minutes.

Recipe Courtesy: Little Old Lightkeeper

Cape Henlopen Lighthouse
Lewes, Delaware

U.S. Coast Guard Collection

Cape Henlopen Lighthouse is not remembered for it's 161 years of faithful service guiding ships into Delaware Bay. Rather the event that holds the public attention is its spectacular collapse on April 26, 1926. When the lighthouse fell, it was the second oldest lighthouse in the United States, constructed in 1767.

Funding for the lighthouse came from a series of public lotteries held in Philadelphia. The colonists recognized the importance of the beacon at the foot of Delaware Bay, especially considering ships had to round the cape to make their way to the Philadelphia docks. The lottery was an easy way to pay for it.

The octagonal tower stood 69-feet high and was made of granite shipped in from northern Delaware. The light was located about a quarter mile from the water, in a pine and cedar forest. It was a place the builders considered safe from all natural disasters.

The sand banks off Cape Henlopen continued to shift and to provide additional help to sailors, a 45-foot stone beacon was built three-quarters of a mile north of the old light. The Cape Henlopen keeper was expected to maintain both lights. In 1865 the smaller beacon was dismantled and another one built further from the light.

The hunger of the ocean is relentless and Cape Henlopen eroded at a rate of three to five feet a year. As the sea moved closer to the lighthouse, efforts were made to prevent the erosion. Gravel and pine logs were dumped on the beach and vegetation planted to stop the water. Seawalls, groins, bulkheads and jetties were also built. All were generally ineffective. Finally, when it was inevitable the light would be lost, the lens was removed. The light itself had already been discontinued. The newer Brandywine Light assumed its work.

When the final collapse came, it was expected but still surprising. The light had stood so long; it was hard to believe it would finally fall. An eyewitness explained, "The lighthouse seemed to be leaning more than usual and it suddenly crumpled into three sections and fell onto the beach." It was claimed many local people went out to the site and salvaged stone for use in fireplaces and chimneys.

Cream Of Oyster Stew–Historic

4 tablespoons butter

1/2 cup chopped celery

1/2 cup chopped onion

1/2 cup diced carrots

1/4 teaspoon white pepper

1 (10-12 ounce) can cream of mushroom soup

1/2 cup milk

1/4 cup chopped parsley

1 pint Maryland oysters, standards

Delaware Bay has been a rich oyster grounds since the earliest days of Native American settlement. The Leni Lenape used them for food, decoration and trade. When the Europeans arrived they not only consumed them for food, but also burned them for lime production until laws prohibited the practice.

Melt butter in a 2-quart saucepan. Sauté celery, onion and carrots in melted butter for 5 minutes. Add white pepper, mushroom soup and milk, stirring until smooth. Heat to low simmer. Add parsley and oysters. Heat until oysters are plump and begin to ruffle. Serve immediately. Yield: 5 cups (4 servings).

Recipe Courtesy: Little Old Lightkeeper

Fenwick Island Lighthouse
Fenwick Island, Delaware

U.S. Coast Guard Collection

Fenwick Island Lighthouse was established in 1859 to light the dark stretch of coast between Assateague and Cape Henlopen. The light warned shipping clear of a dangerous reef known as Fenwick Shoals that extends five-six miles off the Delaware coast. It was also a major aid for shipping entering Delaware Bay from Europe. The two-story frame keeper's house is Gothic in style. A 1940s generator house is nearby.

The lighthouse is unique because it sits exactly on the eastern end of the famous Mason-Dixon Line, the division between Delaware and Maryland, surveyed in 1751, and the historic border between north and south during the Civil War. The original marker stone is still on the site.

The white brick tower is 84 feet high and still has the original third order Fresnel. The light was automated in 1940. Although the Coast Guard decommissioned the light in 1978, the Friends of the Lighthouse, Inc. presently operate the station as a museum.

Planked Shad–Historic

Once commonplace in the river basins along the Atlantic coast, the lowly American shad was often called the "poor man's striped bass" by the early colonists. They claimed only a poor man would eat such a bony fish. Shad are of the herring family and can reach 24 inches in length. The following recipe taken from the *Detroit Post and Tribune* of May 3, 1884 well illustrates its popularity and method of preparation.

"In ante-bellum days, at this season of the year, when there was a long session, a party went down to the Potomac every Saturday on the steamboat Salem to eat planked shad. It was chiefly composed of senators and representatives with a few leading officials, some prominent citizens and three or four newspapermen, who in those days never violated the amenities of social life by printing what they heard there. An important house in Georgetown would send on board the steamer demijohns filled with the best wines and liquors, which almost everybody drank without stint. Running down the river there was a great amount of card playing in the upper saloon of the boat, with some story telling on the hurricane deck. Arriving at the white house fishing grounds, some would go ashore, some would watch the drawing of the seine from the boat, some would take charge of the culinary department and a few would remain around the card tables. The oaken planks used were about two inches thick, fourteen inches wide and two feet long. These were scalded and wiped dry. A freshly caught shad was then taken, scaled, split open down the back, cleaned, washed and dried. It was then spread out on a plank and nailed to it with iron pump tacks. The plank with the fish on it was set against a stone at an angle of 45 degrees before a hot wood fire and baked until it was a dark brown, an attendant turning the plank every few minutes and blasting the fish with a thin mixture of melted butter and flour. Meanwhile an experienced cook was frying fresh shad roe in a mixture of eggs and cracker dust at another fire, where sweet and Irish potatoes were being roasted in the ashes. On one occasion, Mr. Webster, who had some codfish sent to him in ice on a government steamer from Boston, carried them down a shad bake, with a large kettle, some pork, some ship biscuit, some milk and some onions and had a chowder made by a couple of us who were from Massachusetts. He was very particular in having the pork first cut first into dice, fried and then taken with a screen. The melted pork fat remained in the kettle and in it were placed successive layers of fish, crackers, onions and potatoes until the kettle was two-thirds full, when we poured in a generous quantity of milk. I regret to say that the chowder was slightly burnt and was not a success, although Mr. Webster persisted in calling it excellent and ate several platefuls. The planked shad meanwhile, were served on the planks on which they had been cooked, each person having a plank and picking out the portions, which he liked the best, breaking up his roast potato on the warm shad, while the roe was served to those who wished for it. After the fish came punch and cigars and then they re-embarked and the bows of the steamer were turned toward Washington. When opposite Alexandria an account was made of the wine and liquor which had been drunk and an assessment was levied, which generally amounted to about $3.00 each. I never saw a person intoxicated at one of those shad-bakes, nor heard any quarreling. The festivity at one of them however was marred by the accidental falling overboard of a young man from Georgetown who was drowned.

Recipe Courtesy: Detroit Post and Tribune, May 3, 1884

Turkey Point Lighthouse
Turkey Point, Maryland

U.S. Coast Guard Collection

Turkey Point Lighthouse is best remembered for Fannie May Salter, the light's last keeper and the last female lightkeeper in the Coast Guard. When she retired in 1947, it was the end of an era, not just for Turkey Point Lighthouse, but also for the nation.

Turkey Point Lighthouse is located on 100-foot bluff overlooking the Chesapeake and Delaware Canal in the upper part of Chesapeake Bay. It was the highest lighthouse of the 74 on the bay.

The need for the light was recognized as early as 1812 but it was not until 1833 it was finally built. It was a very typical small station consisting of a 35-foot high tower, keeper's house, bell house, oil house and other minor out buildings. Its mission was to guide ships into the newly finished Chesapeake and Delaware Canal. This 14-mile waterway connects the Delaware River with Chesapeake Bay, saving ships a 300-mile trip.

Fannie May Salter came to the light in 1919 when her husband Clarence became keeper. When he died in 1925 she took his place, not only in keeping the light but also in raising their six children, tending the vegetable garden and husbanding a small number of sheep and fowl. The fog bell gave Mrs. Salter more trouble than the old oil lamp. One foggy night during World War II, the automatic bell mechanism broke. Since she could hear the foghorn of a nearby vessel in her channel she had no choice but to manually ring the bell every fifteen seconds for nearly an hour, until the ship passed the light. A few years later the mechanism again failed and again she could hear the horns of vessels in the bay. This time she had to ring the bell for most of the night. The light was electrified in 1943. Prior to then she had to manually fill and maintain the oil lamps, just as keepers had done for a hundred years.

Fannie May Salter was not the only female keeper at Turkey Point. Elizabeth Lusby served 1844-61 after the death of her husband keeper Robert. Rebecca Crouch held the job from 1895-1919 after the death of her keeper husband John.

Today the light is totally automated with electric power provided by a bank of batteries and solar panels. The Coast Guard tore down the keeper's house in 1948 and all that remains of the station is the tower and oil house. The property is now part of the Maryland's Elk Neck State Park.

Shrimp Waterloo–Contemporary

8-10 large shrimp

Dash of lemon juice

2 teaspoons oil

1/4 cup dry vermouth

1-2 crushed garlic cloves

Minced parsley

1/2 cup white wine

Sprinkle shrimp with lemon, salt and pepper to taste. Heat pan and add 2 teaspoons oil and 1-2 teaspoons butter. Add seasoned shrimp and sauté on both sides until pink. Add 1/4 cup dry vermouth and ignite it. Flambé the shrimp. Remove shrimp immediately after flame has died and keep warm.

Add 1 teaspoon butter to pan. Sauté 1-2 crushed garlic gloves, minced parsley, minced dill or thyme if desired. Pour in 1/2 cup white wine, dash of lemon juice. Reduce sauce to half. Stir 1/4 cup butter in sauce. Salt and pepper to taste. Add shrimp and heat but do not boil sauce. Place sauce on plates and arrange shrimp. Serve with rice and asparagus.

Recipe Courtesy: Theresa Kramer, Waterloo Country Inn, 28822 Mt. Vernon Road, Princess Anne, Maryland, 21853, www.waterloocountryinn.com

Assateague Lighthouse
Chincoteague, Virginia

Assateague Lighthouse

Author's Collection

The first lighthouse on Assateague Island was built in 1833. It was determined to be inadequate in 1851 and was replaced in 1867 by the present 142-foot tall brick tower. Built on a 22-foot high hill, it has focal plane of 154 feet. The light is important because it marks the Winter Quarters Shoals, which extend 12 miles offshore and are very hazardous to shipping.

The original lens for the second tower was a first order Fresnel, however in 1963 the Coast Guard automated the light, removing the lens and replacing it with a DBC-334 aero-beacon. The old Fresnel is on display at the Oyster and Maritime Museum in Chincoteague.

Assateague Island is 37 miles long and is located in the Chincoteague National Wildlife Refuge. It stretches from Ocean City Inlet in Maryland to Chincoteague Inlet in Virginia and is a naturalist's paradise. More than 200 species of birds call the island home. Unlike the lights at Cape Charles which where always threatened by the encroaching sea, at Assateague, the reverse is true. When first built, the lighthouse was at the southern tip of the island. But the constant depositing of sand over the years has added land to the lower part of the island, having the effect of pushing the lighthouse far inland. Assateague Island is also the home of a unique herd of wild horses. Legend claims they descended from Mustangs that survived a Spanish shipwreck.

Walnut Greens With Chicken Dried Plums And Spiced Pecans–Contemporary

Spiced Pecans:

1 cup pecan halves

1 tablespoon vegetable oil

1 tablespoon packed brown sugar

1/4 teaspoon ground red pepper

1/4 teaspoon ground cumin

Salad:

8 cups mixed salad greens

1 package (6 ounces) fully cooked chicken strips

1-1/2 cups green beans, blanched

1 cup coarsely chopped dried plums

1/2 cup Apple Walnut Vinaigrette or prepared red wine vinaigrette

1/2 cup (4 ounces) crumbled goat cheese

Heat oven to 300 degrees. For pecans: in medium bowl, combine all ingredients; toss to coat. Bake, in even layer on baking sheet, 10 to 12 minutes or until lightly browned, stirring occasionally; set aside. For Salad: In large bowl, combine mixed greens, chicken, green beans, dried plums and Spiced Pecans. Drizzle with Apple Walnut Vinaigrette; toss to coat. Sprinkle with goat cheese; serve immediately.

Apple Walnut Vinaigrette: In blender, process 1/2 of a peeled, cored and cut-up Granny Smith apple, 1 peeled shallot, 1/4 cup apple cider vinegar and 1 teaspoon sugar until smooth. With motor running, slowly add 2/3 cup vegetable oil and 1/3 cup walnut oil until creamy. Season with salt and pepper, as desired. Store covered, in refrigerator for up to 3 days.

Tip: To blanch green beans, cook in salted boiling water just until crisp-tender. Drain; immediately drop into ice water to cool. Drain.

Recipe Courtesy: California Dried Plum Board, created by Gale Gand

Cape Charles Lighthouse
Smith Island, Virginia

National Archives

Cape Charles Light is considered one of the most important aids in the Chesapeake Bay area. Situated on Smith Island, it marks the north shore at the mouth of the bay. The first light was built in 1827 but its 60-foot tower was considered too short and in 1856 Congress appropriated $35,000 to build a new lighthouse a mile and a quarter to the southwest. The new 150-foot tower was still under construction when the Civil War started and the Confederates removed the lens apparatus and damaged the tower to prevent Union use. After the Union forces liberated the area, the lighthouse was finished in 1864.

Erosion proved the lighthouse's undoing. By 1885, the sea was within 124 feet of the keeper's house and 225 feet of the tower. The Lighthouse Service tried to arrest the loss with jetties, but they were ineffective.

Recognizing the inevitable, in 1890, $150,000 was appropriated for a new light. The third tower, made of iron cylinders supported by an iron web framework, was built three-quarters mile inland from the old tower. Mosquitoes, storms and shipwreck all slowed construction and it was not until August 15, 1895 that the first order Fresnel was finally exhibited.

The light was automated in 1963 and the Fresnel removed and replaced with an aero-beacon. The lens is on exhibit at the Mariners Museum in Newport News, Virginia. The light is still active and is visible for 24 miles.

Lump Crab Meat Dip~Contemporary

1/4 cup cream

2 tablespoons mayonnaise

1/2 teaspoon salt

Dash of Tabasco sauce

1/4 cup lemon juice

2 sliced green onions and tops

1 teaspoon Worcester sauce

8 ounce cream cheese

1 pound lump crabmeat

Blue crabs are found in sheltered bays in the brackish water of estuaries and river mouths. They can be harvested one at a time using handlines baited with fish heads or chicken necks, caught in traps or scooped in nets. Once cooked, crab meat is "picked out" much as lobster meat. "Lump" crab refers to the largest pieces of crab.

Blend together until smooth all ingredients except the crabmeat. Add crabmeat and serve with raw vegetables such as green peppers, radishes, celery and cauliflower buds.

Recipe Courtesy: The Crab Place, http://www.crabplace.com

Cape Henry Lighthouse
Cape Henry, Virginia

National Archives

The waters off the Virginia Capes have always been very dangerous for shipping. Fog often obscures the entrance of Chesapeake Bay and rough seas and shifting shoals compound the peril.

The colonial governments of both Virginia and Maryland recognized the danger and in 1772-1773 allocated funding to start construction of a lighthouse on Cape Henry. Some work began but when the Revolutionary War started, but funding priorities changed and the lighthouse project was "put on the back burner."

After the War, the new government acted to assume the responsibility for lights and Alexander Hamilton, Secretary of the Treasury, contracted with John McComb Jr. of New York City to build the light. The contract stipulated an octagonal tower rising 72 feet from the water table to the top of the stonework. A two-story keeper's house was included. The final cost was $17,700, $2,500 over the original estimate. In October 1792, President Washington appointed Laban Goffigan as the first keeper. The lamps initially burned fish oil instead of the more normal whale oil.

During the Civil War, Confederate soldiers damaged the light to make it useless for the Union. By 1863 Union forces drove off the Confederates and repaired the light. In 1872 inspectors discovered that there were major cracks in six of the eight tower faces. Evidently they were caused by the general instability of the ground. The experts recommended the tower be abandoned.

Congress acted in 1878 and appropriated $75,000 for a new lighthouse 350 feet southeast of the old tower. The new light was first illuminated on December 15, 1881. Instead of being torn down as was normal, the old tower was left up as a daymark. Because of its historical significance, as well as being the site of the first landing by English colonists in Virginia, the Association for the Preservation of Virginia Antiquities became interested in the light. In 1930 the lighthouse, by Act of Congress, was deeded to the Association. Today the old light is open to the public during the spring, summer and fall.

Oyster Stew–Historic

2-1/2 tablespoons fresh bacon fat

1 pound onions

2 pints fresh oysters

3 cups milk

Parsley and onion tops

This basic recipe for oyster stew is solid in it's simplicity and reflects the style of home cooking common to keepers of a century ago.

Start by putting fat in a 3-quart saucepan and when hot, adding chopped onions. Cook onions on slow flame until clear but not brown. Add oysters, with liquid, and cook until oysters curl. Add a handful of chopped onion tops, parsley and hot milk. Serve immediately. Yield: 4 servings.

Recipe Courtesy: The Old Lightkeeper

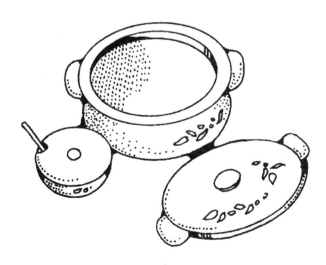

New Point Comfort Lighthouse
Mathews County, Virginia

Author's Collection

As American sea borne commerce increased following the Revolution, the Chesapeake Bay area became increasingly important and the need to provide lighthouses critical. Cape Henry Lighthouse marked the entrance to the bay, but lights in the bay were needed too.

After Elzy Burroughs finished rebuilding the 54-foot high Old Point Comfort Lighthouse in 1802, he proposed to construct another at New Point Comfort, deeper into the bay. New Point Comfort was a narrow peninsula that marked the natural boundary between Chesapeake and Mobjack Bays. The light would warn mariners away from nearby shoals. Burroughs' proposal was accepted and the 63-foot high octagonal tower was first illuminated on January 17, 1805. Visible for 12 miles, the light was an important aid for vessels north bound on the bay. The old lamp and reflector apparatus were replaced with a fourth order Fresnel in 1855. During the Civil War, Confederate forces rendered the light inoperative and following the War, extensive repairs were necessary and a new lens installed.

Since the lighthouse was built on a narrow peninsula of land, mostly sand, the location was dangerously exposed to the effects of wind and wave. In 1847 a series of northeast storms began to cut away at the land, forming an inlet at the base of the peninsula. By 1852 the peninsula was an island. Severe storms in 1933 badly damaged the lighthouse and eroded a considerable amount of the foundation. Repairs were quickly made.

The area around the lighthouse was a beautiful setting and by the turn of the century, it was a popular place for picnics and yachting parties. Commercial fish houses and piers were built to the west of the light for the busy fish trade. Blue crabs, oysters, crabs and various fish were harvested, processed and shipped.

The oil lamps for the Fresnel were replaced with an automatic acetylene gas system in 1919 and with electricity in 1950. Progress marches on and in 1963 the Coast Guard built a new beacon 1,050 yards southeast of the light. Known as New Point Comfort Split Light, it more accurately marks the shoals.

The light was designated a National Historic Landmark in 1972 and acquired by Mathews County in 1975. The New Point Comfort Restoration Committee has worked hard to restore the light and in 1999 a solar powered beacon was added to the tower.

Blue Crab Balls–Contemporary

1 pound crab meat

1 egg

2 slices bread (bread crumbs)

2 tablespoons mayonnaise

1/2 teaspoon Worcestershire

1 tablespoon mustard

1 teaspoon Old Bay Seafood seasoning (may use 2 teaspoons)

1 teaspoon minced onion

Salt and pepper

Blue crab is a remarkable seafood. It can be made into a salad, soup, stew, dip, casserole, cakes, deviled, quiche, etc. The list is limited only by your imagination.

Beat egg. Add remaining ingredients. Mix with crabmeat. Shape into balls and fry in oil. May be rolled in fine breadcrumbs before frying. Also can be baked.

Recipe Courtesy: Julie A. Kaylor, Mathews, Virginia, 23109

Thimble Shoals Lighthouse
Hampton Roads, Virginia

U.S. Coast Guard Collection

Some mariners consider this light to be the most important in Chesapeake Bay. It is located on the eastern tip of Thimble Shoals, just east of Old Point Comfort and marks the entrance to Hampton Roads.

The fist light at the shoals was in the form of a lightship. In 1872, it was replaced by a screw pile lighthouse. There were more screw pile lights in the Chesapeake Bay area than anywhere else in the world with 42 built between 1850-1900. The design called for a series of iron legs to be screwed into the bottom in a rough hexagonal pattern. A wooden cottage for the keepers with a center light tower was attached to the top of the piles.

In October 1880, a fire of unknown origin destroyed the lighthouse. By luck, the lighthouse depot in Baltimore had a disassembled screw pile lighthouse intended for Bells Rock, Virginia. After divers recovered the lens from the underwater debris, the spare screw pile was quickly constructed and illuminated on Christmas Eve.

The Thimble Shoals Light seemed to be a magnet for ships. In March 1891, it was struck and damaged by a steamer. Seven years later a coal barge hit it causing extensive damage. The coup de grace came on December 27, 1909 when it was rammed with devastating results. A storm was raging on the bay and the two keepers were huddled around their wood stove for warmth when without warning the bow of the schooner *Malcom Baxter Jr.* smashed through the wall! The impact overturned the red-hot stove and the wood house soon caught fire. It was destroyed by the blaze, helped along by the exploding illuminating oil tanks. The two keepers hurriedly abandoned the light in their boat. The schooner had been in tow of a tug when the hawser broke in the storm. After a time, the tug rescued the keepers from their boat.

Congress appropriated funds for a replacement light in 1910 but instead of a screw pile design, a caisson type was built. This method required a large cast iron cylinder to be sunk to the bottom and filled with rock and concrete. An iron or brick tower was then built on top of the caisson. The resulting 55-foot tower was extremely strong but expensive compared to the screw piles. The new light was finished on December 1, 1914 and provided with a fourth order Fresnel. The light was automated in 1964.

Crab Casserole-Contemporary

4 tablespoons butter

2 tablespoons flour

1 pound crabmeat

2 tablespoons lemon juice

3/4 teaspoon horseradish

1 cup milk

1 cup grated cheese

1 tablespoon parsley flakes

1 tablespoon mustard

1 tablespoon salt

1/2 cup breadcrumbs

The Chesapeake Bay area is justly proud of their blue crabs. This recipe shows an innovative way to prepare the succulent creatures.

Melt butter in saucepan. Add flour and stir until smooth. Add remaining ingredients. Mix well and pour into greased casserole. Bake at 400 degrees for 20 minutes.

Recipe Courtesy: Julie A. Kaylor, Mathews, Virginia

Cape Hatteras Lighthouse
Cape Hatteras, North Carolina

National Archives

The coast of North Carolina was well recognized as one of the most dangerous in the United States. Nearly all of the shoreline is composed of offshore barrier islands with large sounds between them and the mainland. These islands are also low and without prominent features making it difficult for the mariner to determine his location.

Not only did Cape Hatteras project out into the ocean, but offshore the cape is infamous for Diamond Shoals, running as far as 14 miles out into the ocean. It is here where two major ocean currents meet, the warm northbound Gulf Stream and cold southbound Labrador Current. Their collision causes not only rough water and fog but also a constant shifting and moving of sandbars and shore.

The same 1794 Act of Congress that authorized Shell Castle Island Light (see Ocracoke Island Light) also authorized Cape Hatteras Light. Cape Hatteras Light tower was finally completed in 1802, but it wasn't until 1805 that the lamps and reflectors were installed. The sandstone tower stood 90 feet high topped by a ten-foot tall iron lantern room. A two-story keeper's house was also provided. It is thought the slow construction was caused not only by the dawdling rate of annual appropriations, but also the death of workers from malaria and extreme difficulty of moving the large sandstone blocks to such a remote location.

Congress appropriated $75,000 for a new Cape Hatteras Light in 1867. The Lighthouse Service took the basic design from the 1859 Cape Lookout Light, 68 miles to the southwest, although Cape Hatteras was considerably larger. The Service was very aware the new light had to be the best they could build. The importance of the light was clearly understood.

Construction began in the spring of 1868. It was also a difficult build. The region was extremely remote and as with the earlier light, just moving the material to the site was challenging. The problems were compounded when two ships carrying brick for the light were lost in storms. But nothing would stop the work. In the fall of 1870, a first order Fresnel lens was installed and the light was exhibited for the first time. The new tower soared to 208 feet, making it the tallest lighthouse in the U.S.

By the 1990s the ocean had eroded the beach to the point that the sea would soon consume Cape Hatteras Light. A massive effort by the National Park Service, since the tower is located in the Cape Hatteras National Seashore, resulted in moving the 4,800 ton structure 1,600 feet inland, where it should be safe for another century.

Outer Banks Hush Puppies—Historic

Variation One:

2 cups cornmeal

1 cup self-rising flour

3-4 tablespoons sugar

1 teaspoon salt

Variation Two:

2 cups cornmeal

1 tablespoon flour

1/2 teaspoon soda

1 teaspoon baking powder

1 teaspoon salt

3 tablespoons chopped onion

1 cup buttermilk

1 egg, beaten

"Anyone, including lighthouse keepers, who have eaten seafood on the North Carolina coast probably have enjoyed hush puppies. Corn bread in various forms has been part of the southern diet since colonial days. No one knows precisely when the name, 'Hush Puppies' was given to the small deep-fried nuggets of corn bread that often accompany cooked fish or Carolina pork barbecue. One legend holds that the nuggets were thrown to dogs to keep them quiet when Federal soldiers were raiding the countryside during the Civil War. Hence the name, 'Hush' (that is 'be quiet') 'Puppies.' The ingredients in Hush Puppies varies. Some coastal Carolinians prefer a sweet tasting Hush Puppy. Others favor a bit of onion in the mixture." Joe Mobley, North Carolina Historian.

Variation One: Mix with warm water (not too soupy). Drop by spoonful into hot oil (350 degrees). Cook until brown.

Variation Two: Mix cornmeal, flour, soda, baking powder and salt together. Then add onion, then milk and lastly the beaten egg. Drop by the spoonful into pan of hot oil (350 degrees). Hush Puppies will float when done if a deep pan or pot is used.

Recipe Courtesy: Joe Mobley, North Carolina

Cape Lookout Lighthouse
Cape Lookout, North Carolina

U.S. Coast Guard Collection

Congress authorized the first lighthouse at Cape Lookout in 1804, but it wasn't completed until 1812. The 96-foot tower was remarkable in that while the inner portion was made of brick, the exterior was wood. The boarded exterior was shingled and painted red.

The light was intended to warn mariners clear of the Cape Lookout shoals but as common with other lights equipped with lamps and reflectors was inadequate for the job. Ships continued to run aground looking for the lighthouse! The tower was also too short, which made it difficult for ships to see.

A Fresnel lens was installed in 1856, which greatly increased efficiency, but it was still clear that a taller tower was needed. Construction of a new 150-tower began in 1857 and became operational on November 1, 1859. The Lighthouse Board was very pleased with the result and it would become the model for future major Outer Banks lights.

During the Civil War, Cape Lookout Light was dark for a time when Confederates damaged the lens. When Union forces were chasing the Confederates off the Outer Banks, the rebels attempted to blow up the tower. The only result was damaged stairs. The light was relit in 1863 with a temporary third order lens. Today Cape Lookout Light is fully automated. Although part of Cape Lookout National Seashore, the light is not open to the public.

North Carolina "Down East" Clam Chowder & Cornmeal Dumplings–Historic

2 cups or more, cleaned and chopped clams and clam juice

4 strips, cured pork fatback (strip of fat: strip of lean, may use bacon)

2 large onions, chopped

5 or 6 white potatoes, cubed

Salt and pepper to taste

Adjust ingredients according to the amount of clams that you are lucky to "catch." Add more potatoes and or onions if you wish.

Dumplings:

2 cups plain white cornmeal

Salt to taste, about 1/2 teaspoon

Water

Fry fatback in heavy iron skillet until meat is crisp. Pour rendered oil and leavings into large stew pot. Fried meat is "cook's reward" or may be broken into small bits and added to chowder. Add clams, juice and onions to stew pot. (Note: clams are easier to chop if frozen and then slightly thawed.) Add water to cover ingredients and heat to slow boiling point. Keep pot covered. Cook about 30 minutes or until onions are transparent. Add potatoes and more water. Cook about 30 minutes or more. Watch the pot during the cooking. Stir and add water when needed. Add salt and pepper to taste. True "Down East" people add cornmeal dumplings to the dish.

Dumplings: Combine dry ingredients. Add enough water to make the mixture damp enough to form into dumplings. Pat about a tablespoon of mixture into a flat round dumplings about the size of an Oreo cookie. Place dumplings in clam chowder pot the last 15 minutes of cooking time.

Serve a bowl of clam chowder with the dumplings on top!! Enjoy!

Recipes Courtesy: Jenny Williamson, Marshallberg, North Carolina

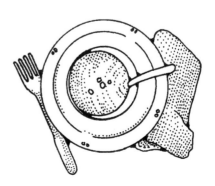

Ocracoke Island Lighthouse
Ocracoke Island, North Carolina

Author's Collection

The original lighthouse at Ocracoke Island was authorized by the North Carolina legislature in 1789. It was needed to help mariners enter the dangerous Ocracoke Inlet and access Pamlico Sound and eventually the ports of Currituck, Roanoke, Portsmouth, Bath and Beaufort. However, when Congress took responsibility for the lights in 1789 the needed light fell into limbo.

During this period Ocracoke Inlet was a major shipping center. While vessels could usually enter the inlet comparatively easily, once in, there was a bedeviling array of shoals and channels.

Just to the west of the inlet, in Pamlico Sound, was Shell Castle Island. Composed mostly of oyster shells, it was an ideal location for a beacon and in 1794 Congress authorized a 55-foot tall wooden tower and keeper's house. It was operational sometime between 1798-1803. The small island was also a center of shipping, including transferring cargoes from ocean vessels to small local vessels, repair and fishing. The coast of North Carolina is always in a state of change and the island's prosperity was fleeting. A powerful storm in 1806 damaged the island's facilities and natural changes in the channel prevented large ships from reaching the docks. In 1818 a lightning strike destroyed the wooden lighthouse. So ended Shell Castle Island.

In 1820 Congress appropriated $14,000 to rebuild the light, or moor a lightship in place. Neither proved possible and two years later $20,000 was authorized to construct a lighthouse on Ocracoke Island. It was finished in 1823 and is still in service, making it the state's oldest operating light. The white conical masonry tower is 65-feet high. The original lamps were replaced by a fourth order Fresnel lens in 1854. Like most of the southern lights, Ocracoke Island was rendered inoperable during the Civil War by Confederate forces. They used the simple expedient of destroying the lens. When the Union reclaimed the territory, the lens was replaced.

Ocracoke Sweet Potato Donuts–Historic

1 cup baked and mashed sweet potato

1-1/2 cups oil

4 eggs

1 teaspoon vanilla

2 cups sugar

3 cups self-rising flour

1 teaspoon baking powder

1/2 cup toffee bits (could use raisins or craisins)

Chopped pecans

If using either raisins or craisins, boil approximately 1 cup of water. Add raisins or craisins and set aside for approximately 3-5 minutes to plump the fruit. Mix sweet potatoes, oil, eggs and vanilla. Mix sugar, flour and baking powder. Combine the dry and wet. Stir in toffee bits and pecans (or drained raisins/craisins). Spoon batter into greased doughnut pans (or muffin tins). Bake at 350 degrees for 15-20 minutes or until a tester, inserted into the doughnut, comes out clean. Notes: Batter can be refrigerated for up to one week before baking. Because the batter is very stiff, doubling the recipe is not recommended.

Recipe Courtesy: Robert and Amy Attaway, Berkley Manor Bed and Breakfast, Ocracoke Island, North Carolina, www.bbonline.com/nc/berkman

Hunting Island Lighthouse
Hunting Island, South Carolina

Staci Jones Photo

The original Hunting Island Lighthouse was established in 1859 to warn ships away from dangerous shoals. Located midway between Charleston, South Carolina and Savannah, Georgia, it was an important beacon for the coasting trade. In 1862, at the height of the Civil War, Confederate forces destroyed the 95-foot tower and its valuable Fresnel lens.

A new light was built in 1875. The 136-foot tower was capped with a second order Fresnel lens. The tower was made of bolted iron plates and lined with brick. Locally it is claimed the tower is a duplicate of the one at Cape Canaveral. A two-story keeper's house was built at the same time.

By 1887 the ocean had encroached so close to the tower and house both were relocated about a mile and a third inland. The house was probably moved intact while the tower was just unbolted and rebuilt at the new site. Following a decline in coastal traffic the lighthouse was discontinued in 1933.

Hunting Island Lighthouse is the only South Carolina light open to the public. The light is located in Hunter Island State Park and a small fee is charged to climb the tower. The shore of the island continued to erode and the tower was moved in 1989. The keeper's house was demolished years ago but the oil house and other out buildings are still on the grounds.

Frogmore Stew–Contemporary

1 pound pork sausage links cut into 1-inch sections

36 inches polish sausage links cut into 1- inch sections

3 pounds new potatoes

Beer as needed

1 large onion, chopped

1 large bell pepper, chopped

3 celery ribs, chopped

2 tablespoons seafood seasoning (there are many good brands, use your favorite)

Salt and pepper to taste

6 fresh crabs, cleaned

6 ears corn, clean and shucked

3 pounds shrimp, raw and unpeeled, headed

Frogmore Stew is apparently a relatively new recipe but certainly very reflective of the traditions of the South Carolina coast. It's history is confusing as reflected in the variety of ingredients. Some attribute it to local shrimpers adept at using whatever was at hand. Another source credits a National Guard Mess Sergeant who created it from leftovers. Regardless of its pedigree, it is a wonderful dish. Frogmore is the small Beaufort county now.

In large pot boil for 7 minutes the pork sausage, polish sausage and potatoes covered with water and beer. Add onion, bell pepper, celery, seafood seasoning, salt and pepper, boiling for 10 minutes. Add crabs and corn, boiling for 10 minutes. Add fresh shrimp boiling for 3 minutes. Remove from heat and let stand for 5 minutes. Drain and serve with additional seafood seasoning.

Recipe Courtesy: Sharon Gagnon

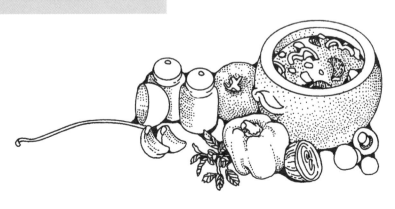

Morris Island Lighthouse
Morris Island, South Carolina

National Archives

Lights on Morris Island have guided ships into Charleston for nearly 300 years. The present light, also known as "Old Charleston Light," has survived earthquake, hurricanes and war and continued to perform its duty.

In 1673, three years after Charleston was founded, a small beacon consisting of a raised metal pan filled with burning pitch was erected at the island. The first actual lighthouse was built in 1767. Its 42-foot tower was far more effective than the old open beacon lights. In 1838 a 102-foot tower with a revolving light replaced the old structure. A first order Fresnel was installed in 1856, vastly improving the effectiveness of the light.

The lighthouse was destroyed during the Civil War by the Confederates to prevent its use by the Union. The present lighthouse was finished in 1876 and first illuminated on October 1 of that year. The 161-foot tower also had a first order lens. An elegant Victorian house provided quarters for the keeper and his two assistants plus their families. About 15 buildings made up the complex including a small schoolhouse. A teacher came over from the mainland during the week to instruct the students. A major earthquake devastated much of Charleston in 1890 but left the lighthouse without major damage.

By 1938 erosion took its toll on Morris Island. When built the light tower was 1,200 feet from the shore. Now the ocean was lapping at the foundation. Efforts to save the lighthouse were made but all of the various buildings were dismantled and the light automated.

The lighthouse was decommissioned in 1962 when a new light on Sullivan's Island farther to the north, was placed in service. The old light was listed as a National Historic Landmark in 1982 and in 2000 the State of South Carolina took title to facilitate preservation.

Savannah Red Rice–Contemporary

1/4 pound bacon

1/2 cup onion, chopped

1/2 cup celery, chopped

1/4 cup green pepper, seeded and chopped

2 cups rice, uncooked

1 (16-ounce) can tomatoes, pureed

1/4 teaspoon pepper

1 teaspoon sugar

1/8 teaspoon Tabasco

In a large frying pan, fry bacon until crisp and remove from pan. Crumble and reserve. Sauté onions, celery and green pepper in bacon grease until tender. Add rice, tomatoes, crumbled bacon and seasoning. Cook on top of stove for 10 minutes. Pour into large, greased casserole dish, cover tightly and bake at 350 degrees for 1 hour. Serves 8.

Recipe Courtesy: *Best of the Best From Georgia*, Quail Ridge Press and Savannah Style

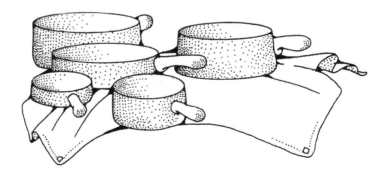

Sapelo Island Lighthouse
Sapelo Island, Georgia

U.S. Coast Guard Collection

Sapelo Island is located in the middle of a chain of barrier islands in mid coastal Georgia, about 65 miles south of Savannah. It is a forlorn and desolate place, far from the stresses of civilization. It is also the home of a very lonely old lighthouse.

Sapelo Island Lighthouse was built strictly because of the small seaport of Darien situated about 60 miles south of Savannah. It was a major shipping center during the first two decades of the 19th Century. Darien was ideally positioned at the mouth of the Altamaha River, which ran to the coast from the state's interior. The river was a virtual highway of local produce.

Ships from around the world came to Darien to load rich cargoes of Sea Island cotton, inland cotton and rice from local plantations. A lighthouse on Sapelo Island was vital to the trade.

In 1819 Winslow Lewis concluded a contract with the government to construct a 65-foot brick tower topped with a 15-foot iron lantern with 16-inch reflectors. A keeper's house was included in the project. The light was completed in 1820.

The light received a new fourth order Fresnel lens in 1854. During the Civil War retreating Confederates removed the lens but left the tower undamaged. The light was reactivated in 1868 and the tower eventually increased to 80 feet.

A powerful hurricane in 1898 flooded the island to a depth of 18 feet and badly eroded the tower's foundations. Attempts to repair the damage failed and in 1905 a new 100-foot high steel tower was built several hundred feet to the north.

By 1913 shipping activity at Darien was in steep decline. Within twenty years it was virtually non-existent and the new light deactivated. During 1938-40 the steel tower was disassembled and sent to South Fox Island on Lake Michigan.

A major effort in 1948 resulted in the renovation and relighting of the old light. The lighthouse is again an important part of Georgia maritime history.

Georgia Pecan Pie–Contemporary

3 eggs

1 cup sugar

1 cup light or dark corn syrup

1 teaspoon vanilla

3 tablespoons butter, melted and cooled

1-1/2 cups coarsely chopped pecans (or halves)

1 (9-inch) unbaked piecrust

Basic Pie Crust:

1-1/2 cups all-purpose flour

1/4 teaspoon sugar

1/4 teaspoon salt

1/2 cup vegetable shortening

3 tablespoons ice water

Preheat oven to 350 degrees. Place eggs in a medium mixing bowl and whisk lightly. Add sugar, corn syrup, vanilla and melted butter. Stir with a wooden spoon to combine well. Stir in pecans.

Pour filling into prepared unbaked piecrust. Bake 45-55 minutes, or until toothpick inserted in center comes out clean. Cool on wire rack. Note: If using a frozen piecrust, be forewarned that they brown easily. You may want to shield the crust with strips of aluminum foil cut about 3 inches wide and about 12-15 inches long. Wrap these around the edge of the pie pan so they cover the edge of the crust.

Basic Pie Crust: In mixing bowl, combine the flour, sugar and salt. Cut in shortening with a pastry cutter or two knives until the mixture resembles coarse meal. Stir with a fork and gradually add ice water until a ball of dough is formed. Press down dough with your hand to flatten it, then wrap in plastic wrap and chill until ready to roll out.

To fill pie pan, place chilled dough on a lightly floured surface and roll it from the center to the edges with a lightly floured rolling pin. Roll to 1/8-inch thickness. Carefully fold pastry in half, lay the fold across the center of a lightly greased pie pan, unfold it and press it loosely on the bottom and sides of the pan. Finish edges by crimping dough around edges with your fingertips, or simply running a knife around the outside of the pan to discard dough that hangs off sides. Press dough edges with the tines of a fork for a decorative effect. Prick bottom and sides with a fork, then chill and proceed with recipe.

Recipe Courtesy: Georgia Pecan Commission, www.GeorgiaPecans.org

Tybee Island Lighthouse
Tybee Island, Georgia

U.S. Coast Guard Collection

Apparently the first lighthouse at Tybee Island was ordered by Governor James Oglethorpe and when finished in 1736, the 90-foot high tower was the tallest structure in Colonial America. A storm eventually destroyed the original light and a new 94-foot tower was finished in 1742. A third lighthouse, 100-foot tall, was constructed in 1773. At some point it became necessary to replace the tower stairs, which had deteriorated to an unsafe condition. There is a story that President George Washington was asked whether to build an expensive hanging staircase or an inexpensive plain set, answered, "...approved with the plain staircase." Lighthouses needed no expensive frills. When the Federal government took over the lights, Tybee Island was equipped with the old lamp and reflector system. In 1857 it was replaced with a second order Fresnel lens.

As normal with the southern lights, Confederate forces rendered it inoperable during the Civil War by removing the lens and burning the interior of the tower. When the Lighthouse Board assessed the situation after the war, it was discovered the station was in extremely poor condition considering the war damage and general construction faults. Inspectors found that fire had damaged the upper portion of the tower to the point that it had to be rebuilt. During the reconstruction, a cholera outbreak temporarily halted work. It was not until October 1, 1867 that Tybee Island Light was again back in business. During the rebuild the Board took the opportunity to expand the lantern room and installed a first order Fresnel lens, making it a primary seacoast light.

A bare four years later a series of powerful storms smashed into the island, cracking the tower. The damage was sufficient that the inspectors recommended building a new tower but Congress refused to provide the funding. Additional storms in 1878 further damaged the tower and an earthquake in 1886 not only cracked some prisms in the lens but also lengthened the tower cracks. Congress continued to ignore the stream of Board funding requests for new construction and it was discontinued in 1933. Today it is operated by the Georgia Historical Society.

Classic Fried Catfish–Historic

3/4 cup yellow cornmeal

1/4 cup all-purpose flour

2 teaspoons salt

1 teaspoon cayenne pepper

1/4 teaspoon garlic powder

4 U.S. Farm-Raised Catfish fillets

Vegetable oil

Sliced tomato

Parsley sprigs

Catfish has long been a southern delicacy but recently folks above the old Mason-Dixon line are increasingly discovering its potential.

This classic fried catfish recipe is a great way to be introduced to a great American seafood.

Combine cornmeal, flour, salt, cayenne pepper and garlic powder. Coat farm raised catfish with mixture, shaking off excess. Fill deep pot or 12 inch skillet half full with vegetable oil. Heat to 350 degrees F. Add catfish in single layer and fry until golden brown, about 5-6 minutes, depending on size. Remove and drain on paper towels. Garnish with sliced tomato and parsley sprigs.

Recipe Courtesy: the Catfish Institute, http://www.catfishinstitute.com

Cape Canaveral Lighthouse
Cape Canaveral, Florida

National Archives

When built in 1868, Cape Canaveral Lighthouse was at the leading edge of technology. It's massive first order Fresnel lens and oil lamps were the state of the art in every respect. Fast forward now to 2002. As America's space shuttles blast off from the Cape Canaveral Space Center the old lighthouse continues to stand tall and true, it's steady beacon still guiding mariners across the dark sea.

The first light at Cape Canaveral was built in 1848. Sailors immediately complained that it was too weak. To see it they had to sail too close to shore, a dangerous practice since the shoals ran 12 miles off the beach and were the scene of many shipwrecks. Another mariner claimed, "…the lights on Hatteras, Lookout, Canaveral and Cape Florida, if not improved, had better be dispensed with as the navigator is apt to run ashore looking for them." During this period Florida was a wild and untamed land. The first keeper, Nathaniel Scobie, deserted the lighthouse during an Indian scare.

Responding to the rising crescendo of complaints, a new tower was contracted for in 1860, but the Civil War stopped construction. On order of the local collector of customs, the keeper carefully disassembled the lighting apparatus and crated it all up, then buried the boxes in his orange grove.

When the Civil War ended, the suspended construction projects were started again and the new light was finished in 1868. The tower was about 160 feet tall and contained a massive first order Fresnel lens in the lantern room. A new keeper's quarters was also built. Originally the two assistant keepers were to live in the quarters provided in the tower but they proved so hot and uncomfortable the men built shacks instead. A passing hurricane in 1876 destroyed all of the outbuildings, including keeper's house, oil house and assistant's shacks. New quarters for the keeper were built five years later but it wasn't until 1883 that the assistants were provided with adequate government housing.

Heavy erosion in the 1880s required the light station to be moved inland. The tower and all outbuildings were dismantled as needed and transported over a specially built railway to the new location. The old 1848 tower was destroyed with explosives to provide material for the new foundation. In July 1894 the Cape Canaveral Light was back in business.

During World War II the keepers were instructed to keep watch for German submarines and like the keepers at Montauk Point, New York, occasionally witnessed the sinking of Allied vessels. The old Fresnel lens has since been replaced with a DCB-224 aero beacon and it is now on display at the Ponce de Leon Lighthouse Museum. The light was automated in 1967.

Key Lime Bars–Contemporary

2 cups sifted all-purpose flour

1/2 cup sifted confectioners sugar

1 cup margarine (2 sticks)

4 eggs, beaten or egg whites

2 cups sugar

1/3 cup fresh or bottled key lime juice

1/4 cup all purpose flour

2 teaspoons baking powder

Sift together the flour and confectioners sugar. Cut in the butter until the mixture clings together. Press into a 13 x 9 x 2 inch baking pan and bake in a 350 degree oven for 20 to 25 minutes. Beat the eggs, sugar and lime juice together. Sift 1/4 cup flour and baking powder together; stir into the egg mixture. Pour over the baked crust and return to the oven for an additional 20-25 minutes. Cool before cutting into bars.

Recipe Courtesy: Martha Nighswonger, Night Swan Bed and Breakfast, 512 South Riverside Drive, New Smyrna Beach, Florida, 32168, www.nightswan.com

Carysfort Reef Lighthouse
Carysfort Reef, Florida

U.S. Coast Guard Collection

Carysfort Reef received its name when the British frigate *HMS Carysford* struck it in 1770. The ship managed to get off without great damage and over the years the name given the shoal has been corrupted to Carysfort. The reef is located in the Florida Keys, just off Key Largo at the most easterly part of the Keys.

Since it is located close to the powerful Gulf Stream current, the reef is a very dangerous place for southbound shipping. Vessels tended to follow the coast, which was unmarked and low, making accurate navigation difficult and many ships struck the reef and were not as lucky as the old *Carysford*. Local wreckers were constantly employed recovering ships or cargo. Between January 1, 1833-December 31, 1841, 63 ships wrecked on the shoal!

Initially a lightship was moored at the reef but given the open nature of the location and frequency of strong storms, it was often blown off station. It's lights were also weak and of dubious usefulness. Manning the lightship could also be dangerous. In 1837 the captain and one of the crew were attacked and killed by Seminole Indians when they landed on Key Largo for supplies. Several others of the crew were wounded but escaped.

The present Carysfort Reef Lighthouse was built in 1852 using a specially modified iron screw pile design. The nature of the bottom made normal piles unusable. The tower stands 100 feet from high water to lens center. A Philadelphia foundry manufactured the tower and to assure ease of erection on site, the entire structure was built at the factory before being shipped with the technicians to Florida. The officer in charge of the construction was Lieutenant George G. Meade of the Army Corps of Engineers. Later, as a major general, he led the Union Army at Gettysburg and dealt a deathblow to Robert E. Lee's Army of Northern Virginia. The light was illuminated on March 10, 1852. Unlike most southern lights, it was not dark during the Civil War.

Carysfort Reef was to receive a first order Fresnel lens but inexplicably the Lighthouse Board somehow "lost" the lens and a catoptric device using lamps and mirrors was substituted. The intended lens was finally installed in 1855.

The lighthouse withstood its share of hurricanes. In 1935 the keepers recorded wind speeds of 80 miles per hour that rocked the tower so severely one of the men became seasick! During World War II the light was dark so as not to provide aid to the German U-boats. Instead of keeping the light, Coast Guardsmen kept a sharp watch for the marauding submarines.

Carysfort Reef was electrified in the 1930s and automated in 1964. The big first order Fresnel was replaced with a third order lens in 1967, only to be removed in the 1980s in favor of a plastic lens.

Orange Peel Preserves~Historic

4 large Florida oranges

Water

2 cups granulated sugar

Peel oranges and cut peel into thin slivers. Use orange segments in another recipe or for eating fresh. Put peel into a 2-quart saucepan and add water to cover. Bring to a boil over high heat and boil for 5 minutes. Drain and discard water.

Return peel to pan and add 2 cups water and sugar. Bring to a boil and boil 30-45 minutes over moderate heat until very thick and syrupy. Remove from heat and chill until ready to use. Makes 2 cups.

Recipe Courtesy: Martha Nightswonger, Night Swan Bed and Breakfast, 512 South Riverside Drive, New Smyrna Beach, Florida, 32168

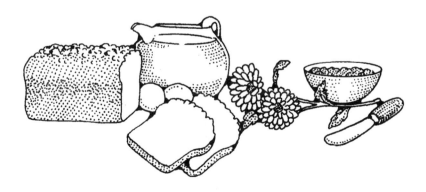

Jupiter Inlet Lighthouse
Jupiter Inlet, Florida

U.S. Coast Guard Collection

As common to most of the Southern lights, the one at Jupiter Inlet went dark during the Civil War. In this instance however, it was the assistant keepers participation in the plot to capture the light from the Northern principal keeper that was critical to success. Once the light was safe in Confederate hands, key parts of the lens were removed and hidden, assuring its neutralization.

The lighthouse at Jupiter Inlet, 15 miles north of Palm Beach, was lobbied for in 1851 and two years later Congress appropriated $35,000 for construction. It was a difficult build. The remote location, various fevers affecting the workers, mosquitoes and Indian trouble all slowed work. Eventually the lighthouse men succeeded and Jupiter Inlet Light was illuminated on July 10, 1860. The brick tower stood 125 feet tall and was topped with a first order Fresnel lens.

After the Civil War the missing lens parts were recovered and on July 28, 1866 the light again warned mariners away from the shoals. The lightkeepers always kept an eye peeled for ships in distress but in 1886 this burden was considerably lessened when a United States Life-Saving Station was built on the south side of the inlet.

The original keeper's home was destroyed by fire in 1927 and a year later the light was electrified. The same year a powerful hurricane caused the electric power to fail and with the clockworks mechanism disabled, the keeper's son had to rotate the two-ton lens by hand. The old oil lamps, relegated to strictly emergency duty by the new fangled electricity, were hauled out of storage and used again. The winds were recorded at 132 mph and it was later claimed the top of the tower was swaying 17 inches at the height of the storm! Several windowpanes in the lantern room blew out and one of the lens prisms was damaged. The hurricane also killed 1,836 people.

During a major restoration effort in 1999, archeologists discovered the tower is built on an Indian mound dating from 700 A.D. The light is currently operated as a museum by the Florida History Center and is still an active aid to navigation.

Pan-Crusted Sea Scallops With Orange Braised Shallots–Contemporary

1 pound large sea scallops

1-1/2 pounds olive oil

salt and pepper, to taste

Shallots

1 cup Florida orange juice

2/3 cup Florida orange juice concentrate

2 tablespoons olive oil

12 shallots, large, peeled

1-1/2 ounces sherry vinegar

2 cups low-salt chicken stock

1 tablespoon butter, unsalted

Scallops

Season the scallops after drying them well. Heat the olive oil in large sauté pan until smoking then add the scallops without overcrowding them. Brown well, turn and let cook over medium high heat.

Shallots

In non-aluminum pan bring orange juice and orange juice concentrate to boil and simmer for 5 minutes, set aside. In a sauté pan heat the olive oil to almost smoking and add the shallots, browning them well on all sides. Add orange juice mixture, vinegar and chicken stock, season lightly and cover. Let simmer over moderate heat until shallots are nearly cooked through (check their doneness with a knife). Remove shallots and let the remaining liquid reduce uncovered to about 1 cup. Swirl in the butter and serve immediately.

Arrange the scallops and shallots around a pile of mashed potatoes in the center of the plate. Pour remaining liquids around plate. Make 4 servings.

Recipe Courtesy: Chef Jim Miliotes of Citrine, Disney's Grand Floridian Beach Resort, Orlando; Florida Department of Citrus

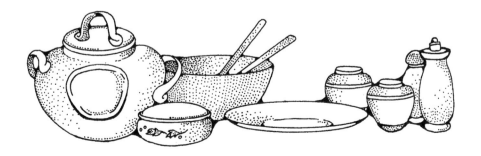

Key West Lighthouse
Key West, Florida

Author's Collection

The lighthouse at Key West was actually built by mistake. In 1824 Congress appropriated money to construct three lighthouses; Cape Florida, Dry Tortugas and "on one of the Sambo Keys." The Sambos are three islets about seven miles from Key West, on the Atlantic side of the island. Construction was delayed when the schooner carrying the original Boston contractor for the lighthouses was lost with all hands in a hurricane. It took a while for the firm to recover from the disaster and by the time the government agent arrived to determine the exact location of the lighthouse, the new construction crew was already building it at Whitehead Point, Key West. It seems the local senior Navy officer determined Key West was far better location than the Sambos and knowing time is money, set the contractors to work. The lighthouse was impressive. The tower stood 47 feet tall, making it the tallest structure in Key West. The first light was exhibited on January 13, 1826.

When the original keeper, Michael Mabrity, was killed in a yellow fever epidemic in 1832, his wife Barbara replaced him. Not only did she tend the light, but also raised six children. It was a difficult life. It was not until 1854, when she was 72 years of age that the government saw fit to provide her an assistant keeper.

Barbara and her lighthouse survived numerous hurricanes but she always kept the lamps of the old Winslow Lewis apparatus burning. The 1846 hurricane was different. It struck with such ferocity, it devastated Key West. The lighthouse was completely washed away except for, "…a portion of the iron posts of the lantern room and some pieces of soap stone…" Barbara was the sole survivor. Five of her children who had come back to the light to help during the storm were dead as were townspeople who had sheltered in the tower.

The new light was constructed in 1849 slightly farther inland. It still stands today. Barbara remained as keeper until 1864, when she vacated the position at age 82. The light was discontinued as an active aid to navigation in 1970 and is presently a museum.

Lighthouse Key Lime Pie–Contemporary

Filling:

1/2 cup key lime juice

4 egg yolks (save whites)

1 can sweetened condensed milk

Topping:

4 egg whites

4 teaspoons sugar

1/2 teaspoon vanilla

1 baked graham cracker piecrust

What can be more appropriate for Key West then key lime pie? The critical ingredient of course is key lime. Originally imported from Asia, they have a unique bitter tartness that gives them a special taste. There is only a very limited zone in the world in which they can grow and the Florida Keys are in that zone.

Preheat oven to 375 degrees F. Blend yolks and milk. Slowly add lime juice to taste. Pour into piecrust. Beat egg whites until stiff. Add sugar and vanilla. Put topping on the pie. Bake until peaks of topping are golden brown. Serve chilled.

Recipe Courtesy: Florida Keys On-Line

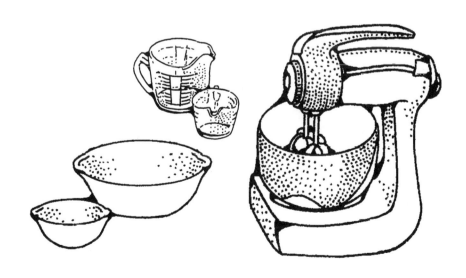

Ponce de Leon Inlet Lighthouse
New Smyrna Beach, Florida

National Archives

The story of the Ponce de Leon Lighthouse is certainly among the more colorful of any of the Florida lights. The area had long been considered as one of the most dangerous places on the coast. In 1565 French Admiral Jean Rebault lost his entire fleet in the area when a hurricane overwhelmed him forcing many of his ships onto the deadly shoals. The inlet was originally named Mosquito Inlet by Spanish explorer Alvaro Mexia in 1605 as a backhanded tribute to the hoards of attacking insects.

In 1763 Great Britain obtained Florida and soon large plantations were operating in the vicinity and a small beacon light at the inlet was established. When Spain regained Florida in 1784, the economy faltered to revive only when the United States assumed control in 1819.

Congress appropriated $11,000 in 1834 to construct a light. The next year the 45-foot tower was finished and fully equipped with 15 lamps and reflectors. The inevitable hurricane struck in October 1835, destroying the keeper's house and undermining the towers foundations causing it to lean precariously. In December, Seminole Indians attacked the light, breaking into the lantern room, smashing the windows and lamps and stealing the shiny reflectors. They also burned the wooden tower stairs. One of the Indians actually wore a reflector on his headdress as a decoration. The abandoned tower eventually fell into the sea.

The second lighthouse was started in 1883 and finished in 1886. Because of its importance, a first order Fresnel lens was installed in the tower. The light was electrified in 1925 when a generator was installed at the station. The name was changed in 1927 to Ponce de Leon Inlet, doubtlessly with a strong view to improving the real estate market. Buying vacation property at "Mosquito" Inlet was not appealing!

In 1933 the first order lens was replaced with a much smaller third order. The light was automated in 1953 and in 1970 the Coast Guard abandoned the light, establishing a new one at the Coast Guard Station on the south side of the inlet. Two years later it was transferred to the town of Ponce Inlet.

Orange Oven French Toast–Contemporary

1/4 cup margarine, melted

2 tablespoons honey

1 teaspoon cinnamon

6 1-inch slices of French bread

Batter:

1 cup egg white

1/2 cup skim milk

1/2 cup orange juice

1/2 tablespoon sugar

1 teaspoon grated orange peel

1/4 teaspoon salt

1/4 teaspoon cinnamon

Heat oven to 400 degrees F. In a small bowl, combine margarine, honey and cinnamon; mix well. Pour mixture evenly into ungreased 8 x 10 x 1 inch metal baking pans. In medium bowl, beat eggs, milk, orange juice, sugar, orange peel, salt and cinnamon; mix well. Dip bread in egg mixture. Place on margarine mixture in pans. Pour any remaining egg mixture over bread. At this point, bread can be covered and refrigerated. Uncover and bake as directed.

Bake at 400 degrees for 15 minutes; turn slices over. Bake an additional 10 minutes. Turn again and bake 5 or 10 minutes or until golden brown. Arrange on serving platter with orange slices.

Recipe Courtesy: Martha Nighswonger, Night Swan Intercostals Bed and Breakfast. 512 South Riverside Drive, New Smyrna Beach, Florida 32168, www.nightswan.com

St. Augustine Lighthouse
St. Augustine, Florida

St. Augustine Lighthouse and Museum Photo

St. Augustine is famous as the first permanent European settlement in the United States. When the Spanish founded the enclave in 1565, it was an important part of their empire in the New World.

The U.S. gained Florida in 1819 and five years later a light tower was established in an Old Spanish watchtower on Anastasia Island. This was the first lighthouse in Florida. Lewis lamps and reflectors were used until 1855 when a fourth order Fresnel lens was installed. However, the beach was quickly eroding and by 1870 the old keeper's quarters and tower were no longer tenable.

Construction on a new light started in 1871 and it was lit for the first time on October 14, 1874. The old tower finally fell into the advancing ocean in 1880. The new tower received a first order Fresnel lens with three bull's eyes. The 165-foot tower, built of Alabama brick, Georgia granite and Philadelphia iron, is the oldest brick structure in the city. A two-story keeper's house for the principal keeper and his two assistants was finished two years later. Paul Pelz, who also designed the Library of Congress building in Washington, D.C, designed both the tower and quarters. The light was electrified in 1936 and automated in 1955 and is still an active aid to navigation. The light station is open as a museum and a must see for anyone in the area.

The lighthouse is reputedly haunted by at least two spirits. One apparently is that of a 12-year old girl, a lightkeeper's daughter who drowned in 1873. Other people claim to have seen the spectral figure of a male in the basement. Supposedly it is the ghost of a keeper who hung himself in earlier days.

Mama's Chicken & Dumplings–Historic

1 whole chicken

3 cups flour

2 eggs

Scant cup water

1 teaspoon salt

Pepper to taste

This wonderful recipe is from Wilma Daniels Thompson, the daughter of keeper Cardell D. Daniels, second assistant keeper at St. Augustine from July 7, 1911-March 31, 1914 and principal keeper from February 6, 1935-December 18, 1943. Wilma remembers this recipe as being her mother's favorite. "The chickens were best because my mom raised them herself and she always had fresh eggs too. I still have my Mama's rolling pin and use it for good luck when I make this recipe."

In a big pot boil the chicken until done. Take the chicken out of the pot and debone it; make sure there are no bones left in the broth. Put the chicken aside; allow broth to simmer. Mix flour, eggs, water, salt and pepper. Flour board and roll dough using a floured rolling pin on a surface sprinkled with flour. Cut dough into long, narrow strips. Bring broth to boiling. Drop dough strips into boiling broth and cook until plump. Add chicken to broth and dumplings and let stew together for about 10 minutes. Yields 4 servings.

Recipe Courtesy: St. Augustine Lighthouse and Museum, 81 Lighthouse Avenue, St. Augustine, Florida 32080

The Gulf Of Mexico

Pensacola Lighthouse
Pensacola, Florida

National Archives

The lighting of Pensacola wasn't considered necessary until the potential of its deep water port and the establishment of the only U.S. Navy base in the Gulf of Mexico was realized. At that point the lightship *Aurora Borealis* was moored offshore.

The first land light at Pensacola and also the first on the Gulf coast was lit on December 20, 1824 and located on a small hill on a site that had been the cemetery for an old Spanish fort. Complaints about the light started as soon as the short 40-foot tower was finished. It was not tall enough to be visible over some of the surrounding trees and thus not visible from the sea. Inspectors also considered the workmanship of the structure appalling.

A new tower was authorized in 1854 and first illuminated on November 1, 1858. It was built about 1,600 feet further west from the original lighthouse, in a location that allowed it to also serve as a back range light for ships entering the harbor. The tower stands 160 feet tall, measured from the ground to the middle of the first order Fresnel lens and is the fourth tallest lighthouse tower in the United States.

On April 12, 1861, the very day the Confederates fired on Fort Sumter to start the Civil War; the rebels seized the light and extinguished it. The lighthouse thus holds the dubious distinction of being the first lighthouse taken by the Confederates. The big Fresnel was removed to render the light useless to Northern blockading vessels. Across Pensacola Bay the Union still held Fort Pickens and the two sides traded artillery fire. The Confederates however had a decided advantage since they used the light tower to adjust their artillery fire. The tower was hit several times by the Union, but suffered no major damage. When the area was liberated in 1862 the light was again placed in service but only with a captured fourth order lens. The original lens and clockworks were later discovered in Montgomery, Alabama and it wasn't until 1869 that a first order lens was back in the tower.

On August 31, 1885, the lighthouse was rattled by a rare earthquake. The keeper recorded it lasted three to four minutes and was strong enough to stop the clock pendulum.

The light was electrified in 1939 and automated in 1965. There are claims the tower is haunted, supposedly by a former keeper. Footsteps have been heard on the stairs and there is also a report of the spirit of an elderly woman sitting in a rocking chair floating in the air 120 feet off the ground! The lighthouse is presently located in the confines of the Pensacola Naval Air Station.

Habanero/Lime Grilled Grouper–Contemporary

4 (8-10 ounce) grouper fillets

1/4 cup olive oil

1/2 cup orange juice

4 tablespoons fresh lime juice

1 tablespoon lime zest

1 tablespoon tequila

1 tablespoon minced Habanero pepper

1 tablespoon minced garlic

Grouper fish can be found in warm water areas of the Pacific, Atlantic, Caribbean and Gulf of Mexico. They can grow to enormous size, but only the smaller ones are fished commercially. This fish is very versatile and can be baked, grilled, sauted, deep fried, pan fried, poached and barbequed. It has firm meat and a mild flavor.

Mix ingredients, except for the fillets, well and marinate the fish for at least 1 hour at room temperature, turning frequently. Grill over hot coals, basting with remaining marinade.

Recipe Courtesy: Jim Martin, Entrepreneur, Perdido Key, Chamber of Commerce, 15500 Perdido Key Drive, Perdido Key, Florida 32507

Bolivar Point Lighthouse
Galveston, Texas

U.S. Coast Guard Collection

Bolivar Point Light is located at the tip of a long peninsula across the bay from Galveston. A 56-foot, cast iron tower was constructed in 1852. Six years later, it was increased to a height of 81 feet allowing the third order Fresnel to be visible for 16 miles. The Confederates disassembled the tower during the Civil War and it was assumed the iron parts were melted down and used for the war effort, perhaps cast into cannon balls.

After the war a temporary fourth order Fresnel was displayed on a wood tower until the new tower was finished. The first light from the tower was exhibited on November 19, 1872. The 117-foot tower was made of brick sheathed in cast iron. Construction was delayed when an outbreak of yellow fever devastated the work force. In May 1933 the light and its second order Fresnel lens were discontinued and replaced by a new light at the south jetty.

Bolivar Lights most famous keeper is Henry C. Claiborne. During a terrific hurricane in September 1900 he sheltered 125 men, women and children in his tower. The only space available was on the stairs. There refugees sat, packed two to a step all the way to the top of the tower while the hurricane winds shook the tower. The storm devastated Galveston. Winds in excess of 120 mph flooded the city, submerging the streets under five feet of water. Nearly every building was destroyed. Before the storm hit, there were 38,000 people in the city. When it ended 6,000 had been killed. With the city so devastated, many of his "guests" stayed at the light until they could make other arrangements. In a matter of days they ate his entire months supply of food. Claiborne had also lost everything he owned. When the hurricane swept through, it washed away his keeper's house with all of his property.

In August 1915 another hurricane, reputedly more powerful than the 1900 storm struck the city. This time 60 people were forced to shelter in the tower. The shaking of the structure knocked the revolving mechanism out of order and the lens had to be cranked by hand. The door was torn open and water rose to neck deep in the light tower. Since the storm carried away the oil house, Claiborne was left with only the oil he had in the tower, a paltry two gallons. When it ran out, the light went dark and remained so for two days, until he was able to locate additional oil in the wreckage of the city!

Shrimp Omelet–Contemporary

6 eggs

1 tablespoon melted butter

1 tablespoon finely chopped green onion

1 teaspoon finely chopped parsley

1/3 cup butter

1/4 pound peeled, cleaned, freshly boiled small shrimp

Salt, pepper, and garlic salt

Grated cheese

finely chopped green onions

Shrimp is the number one fresh and frozen seafood in the United States. Americans spend more than 2 billion dollars for shrimp each year for both home and restaurant consumption. About 80% is imported.

Shrimp is also amazingly versatile and can be prepared in many ways. Using them in an omelet is certainly innovative and appetizing at the same time.

Beat eggs and add the melted butter and onions. Add the parsley and mix lightly. In a warm skillet, add the butter and egg mixture. Cook until softness disappears. Add shrimp, cheese, and another sprinkle of green onions. Season with salt, pepper and a dash of garlic salt. Yields two servings.

Recipe Courtesy: The Queen Anne Bed and Breakfast, 1915 Sealy Avenue, Galveston, Texas 77550, http://www.welcome.to/queenanne"

Brazos Lighthouse
Freeport, Texas

U.S. Coast Guard Collection

Local officials recognized the need for a lighthouse at the mouth of the Brazos River well before Texas was even Texas. The river was a natural highway for the produce of rich Texas farmland as well as a major gateway into the interior. In 1830 the Collector of Customs advertised for proposals to construct a light, however Congress did not appropriate funds until 1859 and before work could start, the Civil War intervened. Reconstruction of the Confederate states followed, then a trade depression. It was not until 1893, 63 years after the original effort to erect a light, that Congress finally appropriated $40,000 for a lighthouse and $10,000 for a pair of range lights.

The Brazos lighthouse was a tubular iron cylinder supported by iron legs, much like others common to the Gulf. It stood 96 feet tall and was completed in 1896. A third order Fresnel lens provided a beacon visible for 15 miles. The design was well suited for the area as the light withstood major hurricanes in 1900, 1909, 1915, 1932 and 1961. During the 1915 storm the tower shook so badly the mercury used to float the heavy lens splashed out on the deck of the watch room. The keepers had to turn the lens by hand until it could be replaced. Originally the light was lit by oil lamps but in 1938 was electrified.

By the middle of the century the lights value had declined and in 1967 the land was sold to the Dow Chemical Corporation. The Coast Guard had earlier disassembled and removed the tower. The third order Fresnel and lantern room are on display at the Brazoria County Historical Museum.

Peanut And Tomato Stew–Contemporary

1 tablespoon vegetable oil

1 small onion, finally chopped

1/2 small red onion, finally chopped

6 cloves garlic, chopped

2 green bell peppers, diced

1/3 cup peanuts

4 large tomatoes, coarsely chopped

1-1/2 cups water

Onion salt to taste

Garlic salt to taste

Ground cayenne pepper to taste

The peanut plant is thought to have originated in South America. When the Spanish began exploring the New World they found peanuts in Mexico. Traders took them to Africa and Asia. When Africans were taken to North America as slaves peanuts came with them. Initially thought of only as food for the poor, during the Civil War soldiers of both sides realized the value of the lowly peanut. With the invention of planting and harvesting machinery and the research of George Washington Carver in the early 1900s, peanut potential took off and the rest is history!

This main dish meal is very filling. Serve with noodles, white or brown rice.

Heat oil in medium saucepan over medium heat. Sauté white and red onion, garlic, bell pepper and peanuts for 2 to 3 minutes. Stir in tomatoes, water, onion salt, garlic salt and cayenne pepper; bring to a boil. Reduce heat to low and simmer at least 30 minutes; simmering for 1-1/2 hours is optimal.

Recipe Courtesy: Krista

Matagorda Island Lighthouse
Pass Cavallo, Texas

U. S. Coast Guard Collection

When the United States of America came into existence one of the federal government's first actions was to assume the responsibility for the lighthouses in the various states and to fund new ones as needed. When the Republic of Texas joined the United States in 1846, the federal government assumed its lighthouse responsibilities too.

The Texas legislature appropriated funds to build a lighthouse on Matagorda Island to light Pass Cavallo in 1845 but realizing the impending annexation to the U.S., wisely did not expend the money. In 1847 Congress funded several Texas lighthouses, including the one at the northeast end of Matagorda Island with the purpose of marking the entrance at Pass Cavallo.

The government contracted with a firm from Baltimore, Maryland to construct a 56-foot cast iron tower and on December 21, 1852 the new light was illuminated. Five years later the original contractor added another 24 feet to the tower. Although a hurricane in 1854 wiped out the town of Matagorda Bay, the tower came through well, with only minor damage to the apparatus. The Lighthouse Board installed a new third order Fresnel lens in 1859, replacing the old lamps and reflectors.

The light was dark during the Civil War. Texas authorities believed it would aid the Union Navy more than the blockaded South. During the Civil War, the lens was boxed and crated by the Confederates for shipment to a hiding place, but was intercepted by a Union officer. Confederates later tried to destroy the tower with gunpowder, but the cast iron proved too strong.

When the war ended the light was in poor condition. Erosion was threatening to topple the tower and some of the cast iron sections clearly showed damage. The government disassembled the tower and moved it two miles farther inland and new iron sections were cast to replace the damaged ones. On September 1, 1873 the light was back in service with it's original third order Fresnel. Five years later the oil lamps were replaced with incandescent oil vapor lamps and in 1956 the light was electrified and automated. Another brutal hurricane in 1886 caused the tower to shake so violently that one of the lens prisms came loose and crashed to the deck of the lantern room. The Fresnel lens was replaced in 1977 with a weaker lens and finally discontinued in 1995. The lens is on display at the Calhoun County Historical Museum in Port Lavaca, Texas.

Chicken Fried Steak–Contemporary

4 beef cubed steaks

1 cup flour

1 teaspoon salt

1 teaspoon pepper

1 cup buttermilk

1 egg

1 teaspoon chicken bullion, powdered

2 teaspoons dry mustard

Vegetable oil for frying

2-1/2 cups milk

Mix 1 cup of flour, 1/2 teaspoon salt and 1/2 teaspoon pepper in a shallow dish. In a second dish, mix the buttermilk, egg, mustard, and bullion with a whisk. Add 1/2 teaspoon pepper.

Dip each steak in the seasoned flour and shake off excess. Dip the floured steaks into the buttermilk mixture and again into the flour. Shake off excess.

Heat 2-3 inches of vegetable oil in a frying pan over medium high heat to 360 degrees. Use a thermometer to check the temperature of the oil.

Carefully drop the steak into the hot oil and cook for 3-5 minutes on each side until golden brown. Drain on clean paper towels and keep warm.

Pour all but 4 tablespoons of oil from the skillet. Over medium heat, whisk in 4 tablespoons of flour. Slowly add 2-1/2 cups of milk, stirring continuously. Continue to stir until gravy thickens and just begins to boil. Season with salt and black pepper to taste. Serve with mashed potatoes and a salad.

Be sure oil is hot enough before placing the steaks in the frying pan. Oil that is not hot enough will result in soggy, greasy steaks.

Recipe Courtesy: Texas Beef Organization, www.txbeef.org

Port Isabel Lighthouse
Fort Polk, Texas

U.S. Coast Guard Collection

Every once in a while the government made a horrific mistake when building lighthouses. A good example is Port Isabel Light which was erected on land the government did not own!

In 1850 Congress appropriated $15,000 to construct a light at Brazos, after lobbying by U.S. Senator Sam Houston. It was the last American base north of the Mexican border. By 1852 the 57-foot tower was completed and lit by four lamps. Four years later a third order Fresnel lens was installed.

During the Civil War Confederate forces seized the tower and used it to observe Union forces and ship movements near Brazos Island. The lens was shipped to Brownsville and the area around the light fortified including artillery. Confederates would later wantonly destroy the lens. The rebels twice tried to destroy the tower with gunpowder charges when Union forces approached the tower. The results of the blasts damaged the clockworks apparatus and cracked upper brickwork. When Union forces finally were in control of the light, it was overhauled and refitted and again lit on February 22, 1866. The Lighthouse Board reported it in terrible condition in 1879. It was claimed the lens and lamps could not be kept dry in a rain because the lantern room leaked "…in every direction." A new lantern room was installed in 1881.

In 1887 it was discovered that the government didn't have title to the land the light stood on! During the Mexican-American War, General Taylor established a post he named Fort Polk at Point Isabel. The government title had been based on that location, but there was no clear title to the land. As a result, the lighthouse was discontinued on May 15, 1888. The discontinuance of the light was met with a flood of complaints from local politicians, mariners and press. All claimed it was desperately needed and ships were wrecking without its guiding beam. In response, the government offered to purchase the land and in 1889 Congress appropriated $8,000 for that purpose. The purported owner was ready to sell for $6,000, but the U.S. Attorney claimed his title was imperfect and started legal action to obtain title through condemnation. After five years of legal haggling, the government finally purchased the land for $5,000.

Victory was short lived. The light was exhibited again on July 15, 1895 but discontinued ten years later and in 1928 the land was sold to the highest bidder for a mere $2,760. The coming of the railroads cut local vessel traffic to virtually nothing. There was no need for a lighthouse for ships that never came! At present the lighthouse is part of a state park.

The Chili Recipe—Contemporary

4-5 pounds stew beef, cut into 1/2 to 1-inch cubes (any cut beef will do)
2 large green bell peppers, diced
5-6 stalks celery, sliced thick
2 large Spanish onions, coarsely chopped
3 tablespoons fresh cilantro, minced
4 chipotle peppers, minced
4 large, mild chili peppers, skinned, seeded and chopped
2 (28 ounce) cans diced tomatoes, drained
8 cloves garlic, crushed or minced

Seasoning Mix:
1 (15 ounce) can tomato sauce
1 can beef broth
2 tablespoons Worcestershire sauce
1/2 tablespoon Kitchen Bouquet
6-8 tablespoons chili powder (or to taste)
1 tablespoon salt
1 tablespoon sugar
1 teaspoon black pepper
2 tablespoons ground cumin
1 teaspoon dried marjoram leaves
1 tablespoon dried Mexican oregano leaves
2 tablespoons masa harina
3 tablespoons tapioca thickener

This chili recipe won two chili cook-offs. It is a traditional recipe in that it has no beans (except as a side) and uses chunks of beef (instead of ground beef). Unlike a true Texas style chili however, it contains tomatoes and tomato juice, which are more typical of "Northern" chili. What makes the chili truly unique is that is it baked instead of being cooked in a big pot. Try it. You'll like it.

Preheat oven to 250 degrees F. Place beef, peppers and other vegetables in Dutch oven or enameled roasting pan and mix together (do not brown meat). Thoroughly blend seasoning mix ingredients together in a bowl (mixer or blender recommended). Pour Seasoning mix over ingredients in Dutch oven/roasting pan. Mix well. Cover and place pan in oven. Cook for 5 or 6 hours or until beef is tender and sauce has thickened.

Serve with your favorite chili condiments, such as pinto beans, pasta (macaroni or spaghetti), shredded cheese (Monterey Jack), fresh chopped red onions, sliced jalapeno peppers, hearty homemade bread, oyster crackers and assorted hot sauces.

Recipe Courtesy: Russ Kerlin

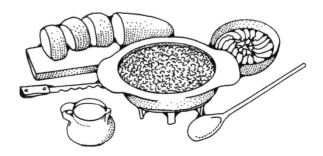

The Pacific Ocean

Alcatraz Island Lighthouse
Alcatraz Island, California

National Archives

The earliest government lighthouse on the Pacific coast was on infamous Alcatraz Island. First illuminated on June 1, 1854, it was a simple Cape Cod style structure with a center tower. Originally a fixed third order Fresnel was used. In 1909, it was replaced by a fourth order flashing lens. A lighthouse on Alcatraz Island was considered important because of its location, right in the middle of San Francisco Bay. The beacon functioned as a range light for ships entering the harbor, guiding them through the middle of the Golden Gate.

Initially Alcatraz Island was the site of U.S. Army defense fortifications to protect San Francisco Bay. Other forts were planned for both sides of the Golden Gate as well as on nearby Angel and Yerba Buena Islands. Most were never built. In 1854 two batteries of eleven guns were emplaced on Alcatraz. The fortifications continued to grow over the years and by 1861 there were 111 cannon on the island. In 1864 the biggest guns in service, 15 inch Rodmans weighing 50,000 pounds were added. At times there was friction between the lightkeeper and the Army commander who felt the lighthouse grounds detracted from the military appearance of the post. It is not likely the keeper lost any sleep over the officer's complaints.

Because of the island's location and essentially worthless real estate, it was considered an excellent site for a military prison. In 1861 it was officially designated as the prison for the Department of the Pacific. During the Civil War it held between 15-50 prisoners, including soldiers, Confederates, local citizens and politicians. Pleased with the result, in 1907 the War Department made Alcatraz the Army prison for the entire area west of the Rocky Mountains. When the Federal government started looking for a site for a maximum-security prison, the island's advantages were well known and in 1933 it was transferred to the Department of Justice.

Meanwhile the lightkeepers continued their daily routine, which included running the fog bell when the gray mists descended on San Francisco Bay, a frequent occurrence. When the clockwork apparatus failed, they struck the bell by hand. Luckily the artillerymen were around with their punch to help the keepers through the "hard times."

As the walls of the prison grew higher, the light tower became shorter and in 1909 a new light station was built providing a focal plane of 200 feet above the water. Attached keeper's quarters provided accommodation for three keepers. When the prison was closed in 1963, the lighthouse was automated. The Fresnel lens was removed and replaced with a revolving aero beacon.

Artillery Punch—Historic

1-1/2 gallons of Catawaba wine

1-1/2 quarts of rye whisky

1/2 gallon St. Croix rum

1/2 pint Benedictine

1 quart gin

1 quart brandy

1-1/2 gallons strong tea

2-1/2 pounds brown sugar

Juice 1-1/2 dozen oranges

Juice 1-1/2 dozen lemons

Artillery punch has been part of American military tradition for over 200 years. Wherever artillery soldiers, also known as "red legs," were stationed, a batch of punch would be concocted when the occasion demanded. There are numerous variations to the punch, usually based on the ingredients available. The common factor was the "kick" it could give the unwary!

Having artillery on the lonely island meant having artillery soldiers and where the "cannon cockers" went, so went their famous punch. Doubtless the lightkeepers interacted with the artillerymen and certainly had a sip or two of their wondrous libation.

Yield: For 100 people (in theory only)

Recipe Courtesy: Sergeant "Short Round" Harry Smith, 119th Field Artillery

Point Arena Lighthouse
Point Arena, California

U.S. Coast Guard Collection

Point Arena is located about 100 miles north of San Francisco. The 115-foot tall lighthouse is on a bluff 55 feet above the ocean. The location is spectacular. The cliffs, sea and sky all combine into a tapestry of awe-inspiring proportions. It is not a welcoming light. Instead it warns sailors away from a treacherous 50-mile stretch of California coast.

The first light at Point Arena was displayed on May 1, 1870. Its powerful first order Fresnel cut far out into the Pacific night. The point is open to vicious storms and winds. One 1880 keeper complained that "...everything not bolted down was hauled around like match sticks."

The fact that the San Andreas Fault runs past the lighthouse adds another element of danger. The earthquake that destroyed San Francisco on April 18, 1906, also shook the lighthouse. The roof to the keeper's quarters fell in and the tower wall cracked. By all accounts the tower should have fallen. Gaping holes were in the walls and the ground was littered with bricks. The violent movement also shattered the lens. Not only was the keeper and his family left homeless, but a frightened black bear appeared on the grounds and had to be shot. The Lighthouse Service immediately went to work and erected a temporary tower using the old iron lantern room and a second order lens. The old light tower is pictured.

Realizing the continuing potential from earthquakes, a new concrete reinforced lighthouse was built. Special concrete buttresses and protruding circular room around the base were incorporated into the design. The new structure was considered earthquake proof. A new first order Fresnel was added and houses for the keeper and his assistants were also constructed.

The lighthouse had a couple of interesting brushes with history during World War II. Shortly after Pearl Harbor the keeper notified the Navy that he had sighted a Jap submarine off the point. The Navy ignored the keeper until a tanker was torpedoed a couple of days afterward. Later a patrolling Navy blimp "bumped" the tower without injury to either party.

In 1997, the tower was automated and the Fresnel replaced with a rotating aero beacon. Today the Point Arena Lighthouse Keepers, Inc. conducts public tours of the grounds. Over 30,000 visitors tour the facility annually.

Abalone Arena–Contemporary

1/4 cup milk

4 eggs beaten well

2 cubes butter

1/2 cup flour

1/2 teaspoon salt

1 package seasoned breadcrumbs or Ritz crackers (for slightly sweeter taste) finely crushed

1 abalone, cleaned, sliced and tenderized

The red abalones that can be found at Point Arena are the largest species in the world. They are extremely tasty! At low tide they can be picked along the shore in Mendocino County. Legal size is seven inches in length and it takes approximately fifteen years to reach that size. The daily limit is four per person during the season. They must be pried off the rocks then cleaned, which requires removing them from their shell, then trimming the external organs. The remaining muscle is an excellent source of protein. It is sliced into thin, 1/4-1/2 inch steaks, tenderized with a mallet, then cooked in a number of ways.

Mix milk with beaten eggs, set aside, heat frying pan and melt 1/2 cube of butter. Mix flour and salt with breadcrumbs or Ritz crackers. Dip abalone slices in egg/milk mixture, then coat with flour/bread crumb or flour/Ritz cracker mixture. Fry coated abalone slices at high temperature two minutes per side and serve. Abalone is great with corn on the cob.

Abalone is also used in chowder, in sandwiches, or may be baked whole. One abalone will generally feed two to four persons, depending on size and appetite. Remember, abalone is very rich. Be careful when cooking ...overdone or under tenderized abalone can have the texture of shoe leather. When prepared correctly, it will melt in your mouth.

Recipe Courtesy: Point Arena Lighthouse Keepers

Point Bonita Lighthouse
Point Bonita, California

T.R. Delebo Photo

Point Bonita is located in the Marin Headlands, at the outer reaches of the north entrance to San Francisco Bay, about two and a half miles west of the Golden Gate Bridge. It is one of the foggiest areas on the coast and a long shoal running out from the headland only enhances the danger.

The demand for a lighthouse was high and in 1853 Congress appropriated funds for its construction. The building of the lighthouse was very difficult due to the remoteness of the location and extreme terrain. One contractor quit outright after seeing the site. A second firm persevered and finished the light in 1855 complete with a second order Fresnel lens.

The original lighthouse was built on a point 300 feet above the sea. It turned out to be a very poor choice as it was actually too high! Sometimes the light would be wrapped in fog but the sea would be clear, making the light invisible to sailors. The only solution was to lower the light.

A new site at the very end of the point was selected. As with the original light, construction was very challenging. Both workers and supplies had to be hoisted up the rocky cliffs by ropes. Rock slides were common. Frustrated by the problems, some of the workers quit. Delays were frequent. However on February 2, 1877 the light was finished. Instead of building a new lantern room, the old one was moved to the new tower. Although the tower was only 33 feet tall, it's cliff side location provided a focal plane of 140 feet above the sea. A special landing platform had to be constructed to allow the hoisting of supplies from vessels moored below. The new tower was so dangerous for the keepers to reach, having to make their way over narrow and twisting rock paths along the cliff tops, that a 118-foot tunnel was eventually cut through the rock to provide a safer travel path. Later a 155-foot suspension bridge was also built to ease travel.

The isolation at Point Bonita was a continuing problem for the keepers and their families. During the 1855-56 period, seven keepers quit because of the remoteness of the station. One complained, "There are no inhabitants within five miles of this point." With the light perched at the edge of the cliffs, one keeper was so concerned about his children falling off, he harnessed them to rope tethers.

George D. Cobb was the most famous keeper at Point Bonita. He is most remembered for his heroic rescue of three men from a capsized sailboat on December 26, 1896. In recognition of this courage, he was awarded the Silver Life-Saving Medal, a rare achievement by a lightkeeper. On September 28, 2000 the Coast Guard accepted delivery of the *George D. Cobb*, WLM 55, a 175-foot Keeper Class buoy tender named in his honor.

Point Bonita was the last manned lighthouse in California, finally being automated in 1981. It is now part of the Golden Gate National Recreation Area.

Point Bonita Stuffed Cabbage-Historic

1 head of cabbage

1-1/2 tablespoons olive oil

1-1/2 tablespoons butter

1/2 cup chopped onion

2 cloves, minced garlic

1 pound ground chuck

2 cups cooked rice

3 tablespoons finely minced parsley

1/2 teaspoon dried thyme

1 teaspoon fennel seed

1 teaspoon salt

1/2 teaspoon freshly ground pepper

1 cup tomato sauce

1 cup beef bouillon

Sour cream or creme fraiche (optional)

Preheat oven to 350 degrees F. Heat oil and butter in a skillet until hot but not smoking. Add onion and garlic and cook until onion is transparent. Remove to a platter. Add meat and cook until lightly browned. Return onion and garlic to skillet. Add rice, parsley, thyme, fennel, salt and pepper. Mix well and fill the cabbage leaves with the mixture. Arrange stuffed leaves in a casserole and add the combined tomato sauce and bouillon. Cover and bake one hour, adding more liquid if necessary.

Transfer cabbage to a warm platter. Serve each roll on a warm plate surrounding with sauce from the casserole. Sprinkle with additional parsley. Each serving may be topped with a dollop of sour cream or creme fraiche.

Cabbage Leaves Preparation
Remove the outer tough leaves, core the cabbage and discard the outer leaves and core. Cook cabbage in boiling salted water; cover, for about five minutes. Drain well. Using cheesecloth, place one large leaf in the center. Place a smaller leaf on the first and fill smaller leaves with one or two tablespoons of stuffing. Close the four corners of the cheesecloth and twist the ends shut. Arrange the rolls in a casserole with sealed ends facing down.

National Park Disclaimer
The wild cabbages growing at Point Bonita are a living reminder of early lighthouse history. They are the descendants from the old keeper's gardens. Like other plants in our national parks, they are protected. Please buy cabbage at your local grocery to make this yummy recipe.

Recipe Courtesy: T. R. Delebo, Sausalito, CA

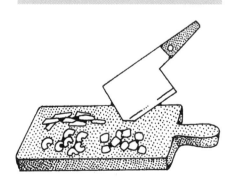

Point Cabrillo Lighthouse
Point Cabrillo, California

Author's Collection

Point Cabrillo Light is about 25 miles north of Point Arena and three miles from the town of Mendocino. It is on a stretch of shore often called the, "Redwood Coast." The light was established on June 10, 1909 in large measure to aid the important coastal trade, especially the lumber ships harvesting the giant redwoods.

The lighthouse is a frame building with a 47-foot tall octagonal tower. Originally the tower held a third order Fresnel lens but in the 1970s it was replaced with an aero beacon and automated.

The lighthouse sits near a 60-foot cliff with a commanding view of the Pacific Ocean. Keeping the light was usually considered a good assignment within the Lighthouse Service. It was near a good-sized town, which meant the opportunity of schools for the children as well as supplies for the family. The quarters were large and comfortable. The only drawback were the cliffs. Occasionally the keeper's livestock would wander too close to the edge and take a tumble. Assuming the animal lived through the experience, getting back up was always a challenge to man and beast.

The lighthouse is now part of the Point Cabrillo National Monument and is operated by the National Park Service. It is open to the public and the third order Fresnel is on display.

Cranberry Orange Muffins~Contemporary

2 cups flour

2/3 cup sugar

3/4 tablespoon baking powder

1/3 teaspoon salt

5 tablespoons butter, melted

3 eggs

2/3 cup orange juice

1 tablespoon grated orange peel

1/3 cup dried cranberries or 6 ounces fresh cranberries

1 (11 ounce) can Mandarin oranges

If using dried cranberries, soak for one hour in juice from Mandarin oranges. Combine dry ingredients. Melt butter and whisk in eggs. Stir in orange juice and orange peel and beat well. Stir into dry ingredients and mix until just moistened. Add drained cranberries and Mandarin oranges.

Bake at 375 degrees for 15-20 minutes. Yield: 10-12 muffins

Recipe Courtesy: Joshua Grindle Inn, Mendocino, California, www.joshgrin.com

Cape Disappointment Lighthouse
Cape Disappointment, Washington

Avery Collection

The mouth of the Columbia River is legendary for the number of shipwrecks that occurred in the region often called "the graveyard of the Pacific." It is one of the most treacherous passages in the world and some sources estimate 200 ships were lost in the area. Open to the full sweep of the ocean, thick fogs and swirling currents, all combine into a deadly brew of destruction. Winds have been recorded at 150 miles per hour, before the instruments blew away! There was indeed a great need for a lighthouse.

The danger of the area was ably demonstrated in 1853 when the sailing ship *Oriole*, carrying the contractors and supplies to build the new light was wrecked on the cape. Fortunately the men aboard escaped with their lives but all equipment and material were lost. Not discouraged, the men were back two months later with another ship filled with supplies. In July 1854 the new light at Cape Disappointment was finished, it was the first lighthouse built in Washington state. A very typical Cape Cod design, it was a house with a tower projecting through the roof. However the 53-foot tall masonry tower was too small to take the intended first order Fresnel lens, so it was rebuilt and the light illuminated on October 15, 1856. Part of the delay can be attributed to having to wait for the lens, which came by ship around Cape Horn.

The light was a major improvement over the method used in 1812 when the sailing vessel *Beaver* crossed the bar. In that instance local settlers raised a white flag and set fire to some trees to show the way to safety.

In 1898 the Lighthouse Board concluded the light was in the wrong location to be fully effective for ships coming in from the north. To fill the gap, a new light was constructed on North Head on the ocean side, to the north of the present light. The original first order lens was transferred to the new light and a fourth order lens installed in the old tower.

Keepers at Cape Disappointment Light had their share of wild adventures. In one instance a keeper was trapped outside the lens room on the open galley during a terrible storm when the door blew shut latching it closed. Unable to get back in through the door, the man climbed down the lightning rod cable outside of the tower to safety.

Today the Cape Disappointment Light is part of the Fort Canby State Park. The first order lens is on exhibit at the Lewis and Clark Interpretive Center. Cape Disappointment is also home to the U.S. Coast Guard's National Motor Life Boat School. This is one of the few facilities in the world that teaches heavy surf rescue operations.

Pan Fried Willapa Bay Oysters–Contemporary

Oysters

1 cup corn bread

1 cup unbleached white flour

1-1/2 teaspoons turmeric

1/2 teaspoon Madras curry powder

1 teaspoon fresh cracked blacked pepper

1 teaspoon dried dill weed

1/2 teaspoon Cayenne pepper

Salt to taste

Willapa Bay, to the east of Long Beach Peninsula, is considered by many as the finest locale in the United States for harvesting oysters. The Shelburne Inn's preparation certainly enhances that reputation.

Mix together all ingredients except the oysters. Bread the oysters in the flour/spice mixture. Sauté the oysters over medium heat in olive oil until they are golden brown on both sides, about two to three minutes. Transfer to warmed plates and garnish with homemade salsa and fresh fennel.

At the Shelburne we generally sauté no more than one dozen oysters at a time in about 1/4 cup of olive oil, then clean the pan and begin again.

Recipe Courtesy: Shelburne Inn, 4415 Pacific Highway, Box 250, Long Beach, Washington, 98631, http://www.theshelburneinn.com/

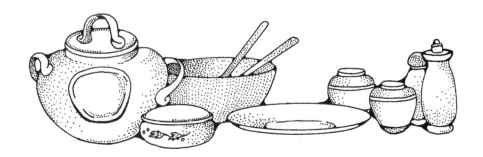

North Head Lighthouse
Cape Disappointment, Washington

U.S. Coast Guard Collection

Originally it was thought Cape Disappointment Light would be sufficient for navigation at the mouth of the Columbia River. Later it was realized the light was not visible to ships approaching from the north. The toll of ships wrecked on the 28-mile long Long Beach Peninsula running north of the cape spoke loudly to this problem.

The Lighthouse Board requested $50,000 to build a new light at North Head. Congress however only appropriated half of the needed amount, which slowed construction. After the 65-foot tall masonry tower was finally finished, the old first order Fresnel lens from Cape Disappointment was installed in the new tower. The lamp was finally illuminated on May 16, 1898. Standing at the edge of a rocky cliff, the light is 174-feet above the ocean. Cape Disappointment Light received a fourth order Fresnel in place of the old first order. To allow mariners to differentiate between the lights, Cape Disappointment was changed to an alternating red/white flashing light and North Head a fixed white light.

Two keeper's quarters were built to the east of the tower. Fort Canby State Park personnel now use both as official buildings.

North Head could be a very depressing place, especially in the winter. Powerful storms were common, often with winds in excess of 100 miles per hour. The dismal surroundings apparently overcame one keeper's wife who committed suicide by jumping off the cliff into the raging ocean.

The light was electrified in 1935 and in 1939 the first order Fresnel lens was replaced with a fourth order Fresnel. The first order lens is now on display at the Lewis and Clark Interpretive Center in Fort Canby State Park. The fourth order was replaced in the 1950s by a twin aero beacon device and the light automated in 1961.

Willapa Bay on the backside of Long Beach Peninsula is famous for it's oysters. At the turn of the century fleets of local fishing boats harvested the oysters and rushed them to gourmet restaurants in San Francisco aboard fast schooners.

Caswell's Hang Town Bake-Contemporary

16 ounces sliced bacon

1 cup chopped green onion

1 large onion

4 ounces sliced mushrooms

2 tablespoons fresh minced garlic

1 quart extra small oysters

1 cube butter, plus 2 ounces

1 dozen eggs

1 cup fresh grated Parmesan cheese

1/2 teaspoon white pepper

1 tablespoon fresh minced basil

1 tablespoon Dijon mustard

Nasturtiums

This recipe by award winning chef Bob Caswell took first place at the 2001 West Coast Oyster Cook-off in Shelton, Washington. Try it and see why the judges loved it so much!

Pre-heat oven to 400 degrees. Sauté 1/2 inch slices of bacon until crisp. Drain fat. In sauté pan melt 2 ounces butter. Chop and add onion, mushrooms, and garlic. Sauté until onion is limp and drain.

In sauté pan melt 2 ounces butter and add oysters. Cover and cook until oysters firm up. Do not over cook. Drain.

Scramble eggs. In non-stick fry pan melt 2 ounces butter. Add eggs. With spatula stir eggs until they begin to set on the edges. Slowly stir in cup of Parmesan cheese. Continue to cook and stir until eggs begin to thicken.

Spray 4 quart baking dish with oil. Transfer all ingredients into dish and add white pepper, basil and Dijon mustard. Mix completely in the backing dish.

Cover dish with foil and place in preheated 400 degree oven. Bake 15 minutes. Remove foil. Bake additional 3 to 5 minutes to allow moisture to escape and to brown slightly.

Remove from oven. Serve at once. Garnish with nasturtiums. Yield: 4-8 servings.

Recipe Courtesy: Caswell's On the Bay, Bed and Breakfast Inn, 25204 Sandridge Road, Ocean Park, Washington, 98640, http://www.caswellsinn.com

Heceta Point Lighthouse
Heceta Point, Oregon

National Archives

Heceta Point Light is one of the most picturesque lighthouses on the Pacific Coast. Heceta Point received its name from Captain Bruno de Heceta, a Spanish Naval officer who sailed past on a 1775 voyage of discovery. Sitting 201 feet above sea level, the beam from the first order Fresnel lens could strike 21 miles into the night sky. Building the light was extremely difficult. It took over 1,000 barrels of blasting powder to carve out a spot on the cliff rock level enough to erect the station which consisted of the 56-foot high stucco brick tower, oil house, Queen Anne style keeper's house and duplex for two assistants. When Heceta Light was finished it filled the gap between Yaquina Head Light to the north and Cape Arago to the south.

For the early keepers, isolation was the order of the day. It was not until the 1930s and the coming of Highway 101 that civilization approached the desolate station. The light was electrified in 1934 and automated in 1963. It is still the brightest light on the Pacific coast.

The keeper's house is now an excellent bed and breakfast. Perched on the cliff it has magnificent views of the Pacific. Paths lead down to the tower and beach. There are even claims that the house is haunted. Some believe the spirit is that of the mother of a young girl who fell off the cliff and was killed. Visitors claim lights turn on and off mysteriously, pacing is heard on the second floor and windows are unlatched on their own. Do the spirits still walk at Heceta Point?

Heceta Bright Bread–Contemporary

1-1/2 cups flour

1-1/2 teaspoons baking soda

1/2 teaspoon soda

1/2 teaspoon salt

2 eggs

1/3 cup sugar

1/3 cup brown sugar

1/3 cup canola oil

2 tablespoons lemon juice

1 tablespoon lemon zest

1/3 cup chopped dried apricots

1 tablespoon chopped candied ginger

1 cup grated unpeeled zucchini

1/4 cup chopped dried or frozen cranberries

Sift first four ingredients and set aside. Beat eggs until foamy. Add sugars and beat well. Slowly add oil. Then add the lemon juice and zest. Add the chopped fruits, ginger and zucchini and lastly add the dry ingredients. Pour into small oiled loaf pans and bake at 350 degrees for about 40 minutes.

Recipe Courtesy: Michelle and Steven, Heceta Light Station, Bed and Breakfast Interpretive Center and Gift Shop, http://www.HecetaLighthouse.com

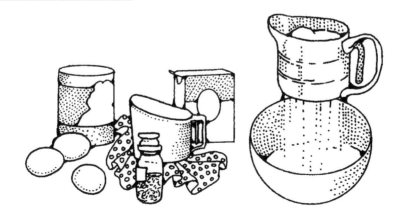

Cordova Lighthouse
Orca Inlet, Cordova, Alaska

Cordova Rose Lodge Photo

Lighthouses in Alaska are few and far between. It has the least illuminated shore of all the sea coast states.

Cordova Lighthouse is certainly one of the most unique in the United States. Named, "Odiak Pharos" which translates from the Latin as "light," it is located on a barge at Orca Inlet, on Prince William Sound, Alaska.

Prince William Sound is best known for the infamous *Exxon Valdez* disaster in 1989. The enormous crude oil carrier wrecked on Bligh Reef spilling 11 million gallons of it's cargo. A massive cleanup followed. The wreck served as a loud wake-up call to the importance of maintaining the unique Alaskan environment.

The barge was built in 1924 in Kodiak, Alaska as the *Berry #1* and spent a career as a pile driver and fish trap setter until being towed to its present site in 1964. It has been extensively rebuilt into the Cordova Rose Lodge as well as the base for the light, the northernmost lighthouse in the U.S. The light was built in the late 1970s by a local fisherman who wanted a reliable beacon for his return from sea. He later convinced the Coast Guard to list it as a private aid.

Nature abounds in the waters off the light. Sea otters, seals and orca are common as are salmon.

Odiak Pharos Blackened Reds–Contemporary

2 large salmon fillets

Zest of two lemons

1 tablespoon of fresh ground dill

1 stick butter

1/2 teaspoon of Tony Chachere's Original Creole seasoning (or your favorite Creole seasoning)

1/2 cup red wine

Salmon are certainly the "signature" fish for Alaska and visitors come from around the world for the fishing and the eating.

Preheat oven to 400 degrees. Coat salmon well in lemon zest, pepper and dill. With a large cast iron skillet, heat the skillet on the stove on high heat with 1/2 stick of butter. Heat until the butter starts to brown, careful not to burn the butter. Add the salmon skin side up and cook for 30 seconds or until the salmon has a light brown color. Turn the salmon over and add 1/4 cup of red wine. Place skillet with the salmon in the preheated oven for 15 minutes (any longer and salmon will be dry). After 15 minutes remove salmon from the oven and skillet. Turn your stovetop back on high and put the skillet back on the heat. Remember the handle will be very hot. Add 1/2 stick of butter, 1/2 teaspoon of Creole seasoning and 1/4 cup of red wine to the skillet, cook on high till until the wine and butter reduce by half, then pour over the salmon and enjoy.

Recipe Courtesy: Gary McDowell, Cordova Rose Lodge, Cordova, Alaska, http://www.akohwy.com/c/cordova.htm

Scotch Cap Lighthouse
Unimak Island, Alaska

U.S. Coast Guard Collection

Scotch Cap Lighthouse is best known for the disaster occurring there in 1946. The light is located on Unimak Island, a wind swept desolate hunk of rock on the outer reaches of the Aleutian Islands. Some mariners called the island, "the isle of lost ships." Russians referred to it as the, "Roof of Hell," due to the many smoking volcanoes on it.

Scotch Cap Light was built to mark Unimak Pass, a heavily traveled passage between the North Pacific Ocean and Bering Sea. It was strictly a stag light and families were never permitted at the station. Duty was so difficult, keepers received a year off for every four years served.

The first Scotch Cap Light was built in 1903 and was the earliest maritime navigation aid in Alaska. In 1940 the old 43-foot tower was replaced with a 60-foot reinforced concrete structure constructed to withstand the most ferocious storms. Direction finding and fog stations were built at the same time.

On April 1, 1946 a massive tsunami (often called a tidal wave) caused by an underwater earthquake slammed into Unimak Island, completely destroying the lighthouse and killing the five Coast Guard keepers on duty. It was later estimated the wave was in excess of 100 feet high.

New Scotch Cap Light was built in 1950. It was automated in 1971. No longer would men be exposed to the loneliness or danger of duty on Unimak Island.

Alaskan King Crab Wrap Sandwich~Contemporary

1/2 cup mayonnaise

1-1/2 teaspoons fresh dill, chopped

1 pound Alaskan king crab meat

4 ounces Brie cheese, ripe, diced

4 (12-14 inch) flour tortillas, warmed

4 cups mixed baby lettuce

1 cup tomato, diced

4 slices bacon, cooked

Alaskan King Crabs can measure up to 10 feet claw to claw and average 10-15 pounds. Found in the Bering Sea and North Pacific Ocean, they are most common in the seas around Alaska. The meat is rich and sweet, a true gourmet delight from the north seas.

Mix the dill and mayonnaise together in a bowl. Place Alaska king crab meat and Brie together in a sauté pan; warm over medium heat until cheese starts to melt. Layout the warm tortillas and spread 1 ounce of the dill-mayonnaise over each. Top with 1/4 of the crab and Brie mixture, 1 cup of the mixed lettuce, 1/4 cup diced tomato and 1 slice of bacon, crumbled. Fold in the ends and roll up like a cigar. Cut in half at an angle. Serves 4.

Recipe Courtesy: Fisherman's Express Alaskan Seafood, http:/www.fishermansexpress.com

Glossary

Acetylene: Fuel used in some lighthouses and aids to navigation after the 1920s. When used in conjunction with a sun-valve system it was the first method to establish automatic lights. The valve automatically turned the gas on at dusk and off at daylight.

Aerobeacon: A modern day type of light used at many lighthouses. It is identical to an airport beacon light.

Aid to Navigation: Any device such as marker, buoys, lights, fog signals and electronic systems such as GPS and Loran used to assist mariners in fixing their position, aid in marking landfalls, mark dangerous reefs and shoals and help vessels stay within a channel.

Argand Reflector: A type of lighting device used in lighthouses that featured a hollow wick in a glass chimney, with a silvered parabolic reflector behind. It was named after Aimee Argand, the Swiss inventor.

Breakwater: An artificial embankment, usually of rocks, to break the force of the seas and furnish shelter behind it.

Bullseye: A convex lens used to concentrate (refract) light, usually in a Fresnel lens.

Catwalk: A narrow elevated walkway, allowing the keeper access to light towers built out in the water.

Characteristic: Individual flashing pattern of each light.

Clockworks: A series of gears, cables and counterweights used to rotate the lens or blanking panels. It works very similar to a traditional grandfather's clock.

Daymark: Unique color and/or pattern or architecture of towers and other markers used by mariners to mark their location during the day.

Focal Plane: The height above the water level at which the center of the beam of light emanates.

Fog Signal: Audible device that could warn mariners of obstacles during periods of low visibility when the light could not be seen. Bells, whistles, horns and rarely cannon, either manually or power operated were all used with varying degrees of success.

Fresnel lens: A parabolic type lens invented by Augustin Fresnel, the French physicist who first established the design, and after whom the Fresnel Lens was named. Fresnel lens used in the U.S. were classified by size into seven orders or sizes based on the lens focal length. The first order lens is the largest at 12 feet tall and sixth order the smallest at two feet tall.

Fuel: Material burned to produce light. Traditionally wood, coal, lard, whale oil, tallow, fish oil, and kerosene were common. Most lights today are "fueled" with electricity.

Gallery: Outdoor railed walkway encircling the watch room where the keeper sat and monitored the lantern and weather conditions.

GPS: An electronic system for identifying position, GPS is an acronym for Global Positioning System. A GPS receiver decodes each satellites coded signal to calculate its position on earth.

Lantern Room: The room surrounded by windows housing the lighthouse lens. It's purpose was to protect the lens from the elements.

Lewis Lamp: A device that used a silvered copper reflector behind a glass lens. The design was largely "borrowed" from that of the Argand Reflector, and was named for Winslow Lewis who patented the design in the U.S.

Lighthouse Board: A nine member board appointed by the U.S. Congress in 1852, established to manage the lighthouses throughout the United States.

Lightship: A vessel used to mark a dangerous area and/or guide ships. Lightships are moored in position with a mast mounted light, daymark and fog signal.

Light Station: A complex containing the lighthouse tower and all of the buildings, structures and grounds needed to make the "light" function. Usually a light station consists of the tower plus the keeper's living quarters, fuel storage building, boathouse, fog-signaling building, privies, etc.

Log: A special book used to record the daily activities of a light station.

Oil Vapor Lamp: A type of lamp in which fuel is forced into a vaporizing chamber and then into a mantle. Similar to the Coleman lamps in camping use today. Also called I.O.V.s or incandescent oil vapor lamps.

Optic: The apparatus used to produce the light. Modern lighthouse lenses are usually referred to as "optics."

Range Lights: A pair of lights placed in such a manner that when they are visually lined up one behind the other, they lead a vessel on safe course. Some guide ships from or to a harbor. Others are used to keep vessels in a channel.

Shoal: An area of relatively shallow water which usually breaks in heavy weather. A shoal, while generally thought of as sand or coral, maybe composed of rock. Water is said to shoal when the depths decrease.

Stag Light: A lighthouse occupied by men only. Family members never lived at stag lights.

Tender: A Lighthouse Board vessel used to service lighthouses and buoys, including transporting personnel and supplies.

Watch Room: A room, usually located immediately beneath the lantern room, outfitted with windows through which a lighthouse keeper could observe water/weather conditions during storm periods.

Wickies: A nickname given to early lighthouse keepers who spent a great deal of their time trimming the wick on the lamp in order to keep it burning brightly.

Lighthouse Index

O-Q

R

S

T-V

W-Z

Recipe Index